Learning and Attention Disorders

Learning and Attention Disorders

A Guide for Parents and Teachers

William Feldman, MD, FRCPC

KEY PORTER BOOKS

This book is dedicated to all children with learning and/or attention problems. It is also dedicated to those parents and teachers who would like to help these children by using those approaches which are supported by the best scientific evidence. —WF

Canadian Cataloguing in Publication Data

Feldman, William
    Learning and Attention Disorders : a guide for parents and teachers

Includes bibliographical references and index.
ISBN 1-55263-115-X

1. Learning disabilities. 2. Learning disabled children – Education. I. Title.

LC4704.F44 1999   371.9   C99-932876-X

The Canada Council | Le Conseil des Arts
FOR THE ARTS | DU CANADA
SINCE 1957 | DEPUIS 1957

The publisher gratefully acknowledges the support of the Canada Council for the Arts and the Ontario Arts Council for its publishing program.

We acknowledge the financial support of the Government of Canada through the Book Publishing Industry Development Program (BPIDP) for our publishing activities.

Key Porter Books Limited
70 The Esplanade
Toronto, Ontario
Canada M5E 1R2

www.keyporter.com

Electronic formatting: Heidi Palfrey
Design: Peter Maher

Printed and bound in Canada

00 01 02 03 04 6 5 4 3 2 1

Acknowledgments

I very much appreciate the excellent work done by Phillipa Campsie. She was able to convert my dry, scientific writing style into a much more readable book. She also did a lot of work digging out additional information from libraries, bookstores, and the Internet.

Contents

Introduction: Only the Best Is Good Enough for Your Child

I have written this book for you, the parents and teachers of children with learning disorders, because I have something in common with you. What we share is a feeling of frustration. Parents get frustrated when their clearly intelligent child seems to be unable to learn to read or write. Teachers get frustrated when a child cannot settle down in the classroom or does not achieve what he or she is capable of achieving. I get frustrated when I see a child with a learning or attentional problem who is not being treated or helped using the best, most effective methods available.

I want to state my position clearly at the outset. *I believe that the only responsible and ethical way to treat children with learning disabilities is to use methods that have been proven to be effective in scientifically conducted tests and trials.* Once a child has been diagnosed with a learning or attentional problem, the appropriate treatment should be started immediately. Experimenting with unproven therapies not only wastes parents' money—in some cases, parents have spent many thousands of dollars on ineffective treatments—but also wastes valuable time. There is a saying in legal circles: "Justice delayed is justice denied." I believe that a similar statement could be used in medicine: "Effective treatment delayed is effective treatment denied." No child should have to wait for effective treatment when it is available.

The good news is that proven, effective approaches do exist for learning and attentional problems. Most of them are widely available, do not involve heavy expenses for the parents, and can be implemented in any school. The bad news is that it may take some time before you see an improvement. There are no "instant cures" in the field of learning and attentional problems. The desire for a quick solution is what drives many parents to waste money on unproven therapies. Unfortunately, there are plenty of people who are prepared to exploit that desire by offering "miracle" remedies that claim to solve learning and attentional problems instantly.

In this book I will help you distinguish between proven treatments based on solid research and therapies that are based either on unsubstantiated theories or on someone's ambition to make money from the parents of children with learning or attentional difficulties. But, first, I should explain what I mean by "proven" treatments.

I am a skeptical person; always have been. When I graduated from McGill University with my B.A., the quotation I submitted to the yearbook was: "Absolutely everything is relative—probably." I don't take things on faith. I'm not impressed by statements such as "We've always done it this way" or "So-and-so uses this approach, so it must work." I like to check my facts, and subject what I have learned to critical review. I want to know the scientific basis of any proposed treatment, and I want evidence that any approach to patient care will be effective before I recommend it.

When I went to McMaster University to teach pediatrics, I worked with Dr. David Sackett, one of the pioneers of evidence-based medicine. Evidence-based medicine could be described as the systematic use of skepticism in medicine. Those who use this approach search medical research data to ensure that there is solid evidence that a treatment has been shown to do more good than harm, and that it is demonstrably better than no treatment at all.

Proof of a treatment's effectiveness can be determined only by rigorous, controlled scientific testing with a large group of patients. Tests that do not use a carefully controlled procedure or that use a small group of patients don't qualify as proof of effectiveness. Doctors who use the evidence-based approach examine medical literature for this kind of proof before they recommend a treatment or procedure.

Now, you might well assume that *anything* published in a reputable medical journal has been scientifically verified using carefully controlled methods. This is not the case. Some medical journals publish all kinds of research, but evidence-based medicine accepts only certain kinds of research as definitive proof that a treatment is effective.

If it's any comfort to you, it's not just laypeople who make this assumption. One of the challenges of medical education these days is, in the words of Dr. Sackett, educating "medical students in how to separate the wheat from the chaff of medical literature." Well-intentioned doctors sometimes make the same mistakes as laypeople in choosing treatments.

Fortunately, evidence-based medicine is gaining ground. Centers in Canada, the United States, the United Kingdom, and other countries now evaluate published research and identify technologies, therapies, treatments, and devices that meet the criteria of evidence-based medicine. After all, doctors need help to sort through the ever-increasing volume of medical literature.

McMaster University in Canada is a center for this type of research. The Duke Clinical Research Institute at Duke University in North Carolina is an important center for evidence-based medicine in the United States. In England, the National Institute for Clinical Excellence (which has the wonderful acronym NICE) acts as an advisory group for the National Health Service there. Journals of evidence-based medicine have been started, and Web sites offer access to information about best practices.

More and more medical institutions are adopting the evidence-based approach, for both philosophical and practical reasons—philosophical, because many physicians and administrators feel that medicine should be a more exact and consistent practice, not subject to the vagaries of physicians' experiences and attitudes; practical, because administrators want medicine to be cost-effective. I think the same reasons would appeal to you, the parents and teachers of children with learning and attentional problems. You want the best available advice, and you don't want to throw money away on ineffective treatments.

You are therefore entitled to the same information that is available to doctors who work in the area of learning and attentional difficulties. If you are a parent, you want to be fully informed about your child's condition and about the best treatments available. If you are a teacher, you need to know about the best possible practices for working with children with all types of learning and attentional disorders. This book contains the most up-to-date information about treatments for learning and attentional problems, based on the best available research. Although I explain conditions and treatments in non-technical language, I also provide references for the most important studies, so that, if you want to read them for yourself, you can do so.

I also want to help you learn how to judge information for

yourself. If you have a child or a student with a learning or attentional problem, you will no doubt want to read everything you can get your hands on about the child's condition and the therapies available. Other books do not use the evidence-based approach to treatment, but they may help you understand how common these problems are. It is always comforting to know that many other people are facing the same problems that you face. You will receive advice, whether you ask for it or not, from relatives, neighbors, and acquaintances, much of it based on hearsay. You will be bombarded with advertisements for products that claim to "cure" all manner of problems instantly—for a price.

The treatments and theories that I will describe in this book fall into three categories:

1. treatments that have been demonstrated to be effective or theories that have been shown to be valid in well-designed scientific studies;
2. treatments that have been demonstrated to be *ineffective* or theories that have been shown to be *invalid* in well-designed scientific studies;
3. treatments and theories that have not been the subject of any scientific studies and that are not known to be either effective or ineffective, valid or invalid.

As a physician and a proponent of evidence-based medicine, I recommend treatments and endorse theories that fall into the first category only. I mention treatments and theories in the second category and describe the studies that have shown them to be ineffective or invalid. I also identify treatments in the third category, but I cannot recommend them. I would never endorse an unproven treatment for any condition, because there is always the possibility that the treatment may one day be found to do more harm than good.

I hope that, in this book, I can impart some of my skepticism to you, so that you do not automatically follow advice or fall for hype without asking some searching questions about the effectiveness of any proposed treatment. You need to critically evaluate other sources of information for yourself, so that you can sort out "wheat from the chaff." You owe it to your child or student, and to yourself.

1
Sorting through the Information Glut

Another typical day: the mail brings me two medical journals, a general-interest magazine, and a book I have ordered; there are newspapers to read, e-mails to answer, letters and faxes from colleagues, brochures about upcoming conferences and new publications littering my desk, and the little flashing red light on the telephone tells me that there is voice mail waiting for me. Current, relevant information is essential to evidence-based medicine, but information overload is an occupational hazard.

I spend hours reading abstracts and journals, looking for studies on learning disorders and new insights into their causes and treatments. In this chapter I want to explain briefly the kinds of studies I look for and the kind of information I accept as valid evidence. I will also suggest a few of the signs that a proposed theory or treatment is not acceptable on scientific grounds, either because it is based on flawed research or because it is not based on research at all.

These days, the word "scientific" is often used in advertising to sell everything from nutritional supplements to new kinds of laundry detergent. However, for a theory or a treatment to be considered "scientific," it should have three important characteristics.

- The theory or treatment must be rigorously tested in a way that is designed to exclude the possibility of mistaken interpretation of the results.
- The results of these tests must be published in a refereed journal or some other forum where they can be exposed to the scrutiny of other scientists. (Refereed journals are those in which articles are reviewed by experts before being published.)
- The researchers conducting the tests should be impartial; that is, they should not have a financial or other interest that might influence their interpretation of the test results.

Let's look at the kinds of studies that are considered sufficiently rigorous to provide valid evidence in medicine.

The "evidence" in evidence-based medicine

Statistical surveys

You can't open a newspaper today without seeing a report that is said to be based on some kind of statistical survey. Journalists love to throw around figures and percentages. However, many of these surveys are unreliable, and I don't mean just those carried out by political pollsters and market researchers.

A valid statistical survey or study must meet certain criteria.

- The sample size must be large enough to produce reliable results.

- The individuals in the sample must be typical of the population being studied.
- The questions or tests must be carefully designed so that they do not skew the results one way or another.

Even surveys and studies that meet all the criteria above can be subject to manipulation. For example, two surveys about the number of poor families in a region may be conducted in exactly the same way and yet produce widely different results. The reason? One survey defines poverty for a family of four as an income of $15,000, and the other as an income of $25,000. The validity of statistical results depends on how problems are defined and how categories are distinguished.

It is also important to be cautious in drawing conclusions about cause and effect based on statistics. Statistics are just numbers, and numbers can be interpreted in different ways. For example, although a survey may find that two medical conditions tend to occur together, further testing is needed to find out if one causes the other, or if both are caused by a third factor that the survey did not identify.

In evidence-based medicine, doctors don't automatically accept the results of a statistical survey. They ensure that the survey was conducted properly and the results have been reported clearly and fairly.

Twin and family studies

One of the best ways to determine whether a condition is inherited (genetic) or brought about in some other way is to study twins and families.

Twin births happen roughly once in every eighty live births. About 30 percent of all twins are identical twins. Identical twins have identical genes, so any differences in how they turn out are caused by differences in their environment, or by what they experience in life, such as illness or injury.

Evidence that a condition is genetically inherited can also be confirmed by studying the families of people with that condition. If a high proportion of people with a particular condition have parents or siblings with the same condition, the condition is likely to be inherited.

Randomized controlled trials

The usual way to find out if a medical treatment is effective is to conduct a randomized controlled trial.

The subjects of the study are divided into two or more groups. "Randomized" means that they are assigned randomly to these groups. No one knows in advance who will be in which group. This is to ensure the integrity of the results. If people who are most likely to improve are put in the group receiving the treatment under study, then the results would not be valid.

"Controlled" means that one of the groups is a control group. The people in this group may receive conventional treatment instead of the treatment that is being studied. Or they may receive a placebo instead of a treatment. In a study involving drugs, the placebo is a pill or liquid that looks like medicine but contains no medicinal ingredients. In a study of a treatment that does not involve drugs, the control group may receive an "attention placebo." That means that the control group receives the researcher's attention for the same amount of time as the study group, carrying out some activity that is unlikely to alter their condition.

The importance of the control group is to account for the "placebo effect." It is well known that some people who receive treatment improve just because they believe that they are being helped by the treatment or because they are receiving extra attention. This effect applies to people both in the treatment group and in the control group. However, if more people in the treatment group improve than in the control group, or if the improvement is more marked for the treatment group than for the control group, researchers conclude that the treatment really is having a beneficial effect.

In some cases, one group in the study may receive no treatment at all. This is so that researchers can compare the treatment to the alternative of doing nothing. Not only should a treatment do more good than harm, it should also do more good than leaving the condition alone. For certain conditions, such as frequent sore throats, time may lead to as much improvement as an operation to remove the tonsils.

Double-blind studies

This kind of randomized controlled trial is designed to overcome the prejudices and assumptions of the people involved in the study.

For example, many people have strong opinions about whether or not certain medications should be given to children. In a double-blind study of medications for an attentional disorder, it is important that nobody—not the teachers, the parents, or the children themselves—know who is receiving the medication and who is receiving the placebo. Otherwise people who strongly believe in the usefulness of medication might overstate any improvements they notice in children who receive medication. Those who disagree with the use of medication might overstate improvements in the placebo group.

Comparative studies

Comparative studies are a straightforward way to assess the validity of theories about the causes of learning disorders and other conditions.

Researchers study a group of people with a particular condition and a group of people who do not have the condition and compare the results. For example, if a researcher had a theory that dyslexia is related to a neurologic changes in the brain, then the way to test this theory would be to do CAT (computerized axial tomography) scans on a large group of people with dyslexia and a large group of people without dyslexia to see if there really are differences in the brains of the two groups.

These are the main types of studies that are acceptable as evidence that a medical theory is valid or that a treatment is effective. Unfortunately, these studies are often buried in the information glut: the flood of information, misinformation, opinion, speculation, and rumor that surrounds us every day in newspapers and magazines and on the Internet and television.

Junk science, pseudoscience, and non-science

It can be very difficult to judge information that appears to be scientific, and yet is based on flawed or misreported research. For example, for years the scientific establishment has been arguing furiously over the question of whether people can get cancer simply because they live close to high-tension power-transmission lines. A biologist in California published research that appeared to show that electromagnetic fields have a carcinogenic effect on human cells. Then it turned out that the biologist had misrepresented his research by failing to report data that did not support his hypothesis. Why? Presumably because as long as his hypothesis appeared to be valid, he was able to get $3.3 million in grants to support further research.

This is not merely bad or sloppy science; this is fraud dressed up to look like science. Scientific fraud is not very common, but it does occur. It is particularly dangerous because it is hard to detect and difficult to prove. Other types of junk science are more obvious, but they are seldom exposed in such a public way, so they tend to persist.

Once a book has been published, it remains in libraries and bookstores, even though the contents of the book may have been discredited in academic publications, or even in the popular press. It may even be cited by others because it carries that status conferred by printed material. You will read in a later chapter of this book about some fairly flaky notions on how to treat learning disorders or attention deficit hyperactivity disorder (ADHD), notions that have long since been disproven by scientific studies. Nevertheless, on my last visit to a bookstore, I could see that the self-published books of the people who promote these ideas are still available, sitting on the shelves next to authoritative texts, and almost indistinguishable from them.

As for the Internet, good information, useless twaddle, advertising hype, and egotistical self-promotion are so mixed up that sorting them out is a full-time job, or it would be if anyone had the time and the patience. When I typed in "ADHD" on one search engine, I was told that there were 118,008 Web pages that used the term. By the time you read this, there will be more. Although I gave up looking through the listings after the first few hundred, there were far more instances of quackery than of reliable information. Bad ideas never die, they just go on the Internet.

Learning disorders are the subject of quantities of junk science, because authentic science still has a long way to go to understand these disorders fully. There is all too much room for unsupported hypotheses and half-baked notions. Fortunately, many of them are quite easy to spot. For example:

- Be leery when an author who proposes a treatment for learning disorders cites only his or her own research and no research conducted by others. If no one else can come up with the same results, how valid could the research have been?

- Be wary of claims that are accompanied by the words "miraculous," "cure," "guaranteed," or "amazing breakthrough." All of these words and more have been used to tout weight-loss programs, and yet people still struggle with obesity. It is the same with learning disorders. There are no instant miracle cures, but there *are* effective long-term treatments. However, they require time and effort.

- Take a close look at the credentials of anyone claiming to have found a "breakthrough" in treating learning disorders. If a study comes from an institution you have never heard of, check it out. Just as anyone can buy a mail-order Ph.D., a group of people can set up an institute with an impressive-sounding name and broadcast their ideas in a self-published journal or on the Internet. Quite a few institutes or clinics have been set up to promote non-scientific approaches to treating learning disorders. Most of them publish stories about individuals they have helped. None of them mention those who have not been helped and have lost a lot of money trying the "breakthrough cure."

- Treat one-size-fits-all treatments with skepticism. If a treatment claims to cure everything from headaches to acne to insomnia to dyslexia, what it the likelihood that it does any one thing effectively?

A closer look at alternative therapies

Alternative therapies are those that are offered outside the conventional medical establishment. They include homeopathy, acupuncture, chiropractic, and herbal remedies. In this book, we will look at a few alternative therapies more closely.

Some alternative treatments have been found to be effective for specific problems. Chiropractic can help ease chronic low back pain in adults. Certain herbal treatments, such as St. John's Wort for depression, have also been found to be effective in moderation. "Traditional" physicians may sometimes recommend therapies like these to their patients for particular problems.

However, certain alternative-therapy practitioners claim that a certain therapy can do more than treat specific problems. They claim that their specialty can solve a wide range of problems, from hives to heart disease, although there may be no evidence to support these claims. One of the reasons for these claims may be that many alternative therapies are said to be "holistic," that is, they treat the whole person, not just the specific problem.

The expression "holistic" medicine has a certain appeal. However, the claim also raises some questions. For example, it suggests that conventional medicine is not holistic, that it is invariably reductive, treating only the symptoms and not the whole person. This is not necessarily the case. "Holistic" has much more to do with the attitude of the practitioner than with any particular therapy. Nowadays, "traditional" doctors are expected to consider the whole person. Your doctor should treat you as an individual and should recommend treatments or therapies that are appropriate for you and that will lessen your problems, not increase them. If you feel that your doctor treats you only as a collection of parts and symptoms, perhaps you should find a doctor who has a more holistic attitude. It is equally possible that you will find a practitioner of some alternative therapy who is more focused on selling you the particular therapy than in finding out if the therapy is appropriate for you.

Another claim made by some practitioners is that alternative therapies are somehow superior to conventional medicine because they have been around for hundreds, even thousands, of years. In response to this claim, I can only say that, during those hundreds or thousands of years, the therapies failed to make the same strides in increasing human lifespan and improving overall health as conventional medicine has made over the last century. Nobody wants to use outmoded technology in any other area of life; why use it in this vital area?

Finally, most alternative therapies are not subject to the regulation that is required for mainstream medicine. For example, the doses and contents of some herbal remedies are not as carefully controlled as those of prescription drugs. Some herbal remedies may contain contaminants, and some may be harmful if taken in too-large doses. Other therapies that involve manipulation of the body, such as massage, reflexology, or chiropractic, may increase the patient's suffering rather than relieving it, if they are used inappropriately. Some alternative practitioners have been sued for inflicting unnecessary pain.

If an alternative therapy is truly effective, its effectiveness can be demonstrated in a randomized controlled trial. When this happens, it will cease to be an alternative therapy and become part of mainstream medicine. At present, however, only a few alternative therapies have been tested in controlled trials, and none has yet been found to have any effect on children with learning or attentional problems.

Let your common sense be your guide

Don't let your anxiety about your child or student overrule your own common sense. Never rely on hearsay. If someone tells you about a new treatment that worked wonders for a friend's brother's neighbor's child, check it out carefully. If you read in a popular magazine about an "amazing" new approach to learning disorders, do some research before trying the new approach. Talk to a doctor. Talk to the special-education teacher at the school. Talk to a specialist. Get the facts before you spend any time or money on any treatment.

Remember: there are effective mainstream treatments for most children with learning or attentional problems. To deny these treatments to a child in favor of alternative therapy is not in the child's best interests.

2

Dyslexia and Reading Problems

"I'm not stupid and I'm not lazy. I just find reading hard."

It saddens me when I hear about children with dyslexia who are called "stupid" by other children, or "lazy" by their parents or teachers. The kids in the schoolyard may not know any better, but there is no excuse for adults to destroy the self-esteem of a child with reading problems.

Unfortunately, some parents who know that their child is bright are baffled by the child's poor performance at school and assume that he or she simply isn't trying hard enough. They react by putting pressure on the child to work harder. At the same time, some teachers these days are so stressed by their jobs, coping with ever-increasing demands and shrinking resources, that they, too, may assume that the child is not making an effort to keep up. They may try to move the child into a special-education class, or simply give the child low marks without trying to find out why he or she is having difficulty.

Diagnosing and overcoming reading problems are not particularly hard to do, but they take time and patience. Parents and teachers must listen and observe carefully to understand the child's difficulties. Then they must spend time helping the child overcome the problem. In our hectic lives, time is often the scarcest commodity. As a result, reading problems may go uncorrected, either because nobody has the time to respond, or because parents grasp at some alternative therapy that promises results with a minimum investment of time.

I have, however, known parents who decided that helping their child was the most important use of their time. I once worked with a family that had emigrated from Somalia. The son had dyslexia. The mother spoke no English and the father worked at two jobs to make ends meet. But when he heard that his son could be helped with simple reading exercises, the father quit his second job and spent hours with the boy, helping him sound out words. Within about four months, the son's reading level was a grade higher, and he continued to improve after that. I imagine the family had to make some sacrifices because of the forgone income, but I think they felt that the sacrifices were worthwhile. I certainly do.

If a child can't read, does that automatically mean he or she is dyslexic?

It's important not to jump to conclusions. Before I define and describe dyslexia, I should mention some of the other things that may interfere with a child's mastery of reading. When I talk to parents and teachers, I try to get answers to the following questions before I consider the possibility that a child has dyslexia.

Is the child unfamiliar with the language of instruction?

If a child speaks one language at home and another at school, he or she might well find reading difficult at first. The children of recent immigrants to Canada and children in immersion programs may find it hard to keep up in a second language. In some cases, the child may be exposed to several languages every day. For example, in parts of Quebec, children of newly arrived immigrants may learn French at school, hear English in the streets and on television, and speak a third language at home. These children may find it hard to learn to read, but they will learn, given time. The problems of immigrant children may be compounded, however, if their teachers have low expectations of their potential and do not take the time to help them catch up.

Does the child have a physical handicap that makes reading difficult?

Children with serious eye problems, children suffering from complete or partial deafness, children taking medication for epilepsy, children with cerebral palsy—all may have difficulty learning to read. Most of these children can learn to read, but they may need extra help.

Was the child born prematurely?

Children who were born prematurely or who weighed very little at birth sometimes have learning difficulties or attentional problems. Premature babies may have mild to moderate degrees of brain damage. This may interfere with learning in general, or more specifically with learning academic subjects, including reading. However, I know a university professor who was born prematurely and weighed two pounds at birth, so clearly prematurity is not always a permanent barrier to success.

Does the child have a history of absenteeism?

Children who have missed a lot of classes, either because of ill health or because of family problems, may fall behind in school. They will need extra help to catch up.

Has the child attended many different schools?

Children from families who frequently move from one place to another may also fall behind in school. Since different schools and different teachers may have different approaches to teaching reading, children who move from school to school may become confused by frequent changes of approach. They may need individual coaching to help them catch up.

Are there problems at home that might make it hard for the child to settle down in school?

Children who have a turbulent home life or who live in neighborhoods where crime is prevalent will probably find it hard to focus on schoolwork. Children also need role models when they are learning to read. If the adults around them do not read for pleasure or do not appear to value education, they will have little motivation to work on their reading or other skills.

Is the quality of teaching poor?

Some underperforming students have underperforming teachers. I have met teachers who don't respect children enough to be able to help them achieve their potential. I know of others who are suffering from so much stress and burnout that they have come to dislike their jobs. Still others may be teaching a subject that is not one with which they feel most comfortable. It's hard to expect children to develop any enthusiasm for reading when the teacher clearly does not enjoy the job of teaching or when the teacher's mind is elsewhere.

Is the child simply bored at school?

A few children who are perfectly capable of doing well are turned off by school. Extremely bright children who are not in a program for gifted students may find everyday schoolwork so undemanding that they can't be bothered to do the tasks they are assigned. Some may have another interest, such as sports or video games, that absorbs them so much that they neglect everything else. These children need extra challenges to keep them motivated. In a large class, their needs may go unnoticed.

Because of these kinds of problems, many children find it hard to learn to read. However, some children have none of these problems, and yet they still cannot seem to master the skill. In most cases, the cause of their difficulty is dyslexia.

What is dyslexia?

Dyslexia affects 5 to 10 percent of all children. The condition was first diagnosed in the late nineteenth century, when it was called "word blindness." The best available evidence suggests that the causes of dyslexia are genetic, that is, the condition is inherited from one or both parents. This evidence comes from studies of identical twins. If one twin has dyslexia, the chances are about 85 to 100 percent that the other one does too. Other studies also show that dyslexia runs in families. If a child has dyslexia, there is about a 40 percent chance that his or her siblings also have the condition. And when a parent has dyslexia, there is a 25 to 50 percent chance that he or she will pass on the condition to his or her children.

Some researchers have found that dyslexia tends to affect more boys than girls; others believe that the proportions of dyslexic boys and girls are roughly equal. I know that in my practice I see more boys than girls. Perhaps the reason for the disagreement may be that dyslexia is not always diagnosed correctly, which makes it hard to estimate numbers. However, one genetic study, conducted by researchers at the University of Colorado, found that male relatives of dyslexics are more likely to have reading problems than are female relatives.

What exactly does someone with dyslexia inherit? Researchers using techniques such as magnetic resonance imaging (MRI) have found that the brains of people with dyslexia differ from those of people without the condition. Not all the studies agree exactly about where the differences are or how important they are for reading. This is because MRI techniques and types of measurement differ. As MRI techniques become more standardized, we can look forward to getting more precise information about the brains of people with dyslexia. However, researchers do agree that the problem can be traced to the differences in the structure, chemistry, and functioning of the brain.

In people with dyslexia, these differences affect what is known as *phonological processing*. This means the ability to make a connection between the written form of a word on a page and the sound of the word when it is spoken aloud. Children first encounter language by hearing it spoken. They learn to speak by imitating the sounds they have heard. When they learn to read, they build on a vocabulary of words they know by ear.

That may seem to be a straightforward matter, but reading is a complex process. Think about it. It involves:

- scanning the letters in the correct order, left to right;
- transmitting those letters, in sequence, to the brain;

- recognizing the distinctive grouping of letters that makes a particular word—this includes identifying the individual letters, in whatever font or handwriting they appear;
- comparing that grouping to known words stored in the memory to identify both the sound and the meaning of the whole word;
- retaining that meaning and connecting it to those of the rest of the words in the sentence to develop a full understanding of the writer's meaning;
- completing the entire process in a fraction of a second, as the eye moves on to the next sentence.

It's an everyday miracle that most of us take for granted. However, if anything goes wrong at any step in the process, the miracle does not take place. For dyslexic children, the chief hurdle seems to be making the connection between a group of letters on a page and a word that they know by its sound.

Their task is probably made harder by the English language itself. Although there are only twenty-six letters in the alphabet, there are forty-four different possible sounds. Moreover, the way in which those sounds are represented is inconsistent, because of the way English developed, borrowing words from many other languages. The same combination of letters may be pronounced in several different ways (for example, *through, rough, cough*) and different combinations of letters may produce the same sound (*there, their, they're*). Because of these inconsistencies, there are 577 possible combinations of letters and sounds in English. Nobody ever said that learning to read English is easy.

When the words don't make sense

If you are the parent or teacher of a child with dyslexia, it may be some time before you notice a problem with the child's reading.

When you read the same story aloud many times to young children, they tend to memorize the words. They can then look at the pictures and recite the story, and it appears that they are "reading" it. Since reading is, in a sense, an aid to memory, children who cannot rely on that aid may become very good at memorizing stories.

Most children start learning to read when they are five or six. Some children learn faster than others, but at this age it is too soon to tell if a child has dyslexia, because all children make many mistakes in sounding out and identifying words. Reading difficulties start to show up when the child is seven or eight, the age at which most children are able to read without help. At this point, dyslexic children become aware that they are different from their schoolmates, because they still cannot decode the words.

The signs of dyslexia are not hard to spot, if teachers and parents are careful to look for them. For example, if you show a dyslexic child an unfamiliar book, he or she may make up a story based on the pictures that bears no relation to the story in the text. If you ask the child to focus on the words, he or she may try to get out of the task.

When you do get the child to look at the words, the child's difficulties will be evident. Dyslexic children may

- read very slowly and hesitantly;
- follow the text on the page with a forefinger;
- leave out syllables, words, phrases, or even lines of text;
- add words or phrases that are not in the text;
- reverse the order of letters or syllables within a word;
- mispronounce words, including familiar words;
- substitute one word for another, even if the substituted word is meaningless in the context;
- make up words that have no meaning;
- ignore punctuation.

In trying to write, dyslexic children may

- put letters in the wrong order within a word;
- leave out letters from words;
- add extra letters to words;
- substitute one letter for another, even if the sound is dissimilar;
- write strings of letters than bear no relation to the sound of the intended words;
- leave out punctuation.

All children make these kinds of errors when they are just beginning to read and write. However, the difficulties persist with dyslexic children. Without remedial training, they continue to make frequent, significant mistakes. Simply pointing out the mistakes to them does not help them correct the errors.

Over time, if dyslexic children are not given help to solve the problem, they will become frustrated and start to dread classes that involve reading. Their frustration may take the form of bad behavior, anger, clowning, or withdrawal. They may become disruptive in class when everyone else is engaged in silent reading. Some may come to dislike school so much that they make up excuses to stay home.

Parents and teachers need to pay attention to these clues. It's not enough to notice the bad behavior without spotting the pattern behind it. Parents and teachers should meet regularly to discuss these kinds of problems and compare the child's behavior at home with his or her behavior at school so that they can trace the problem to its origin.

Sounds and sense: how children learn to read

Children learning to read use various strategies. Visual memory can help them interpret certain words by their shapes alone. The word "little" is full of up and down strokes. The word "people" is full of circles. But visual memory can go only so far. It doesn't help when a child sees a word for the first time, and it can be confusing when two words look much the same. So the next stage is to make the connection between the letters and their sounds. In English, this means learning those 577 possible combinations of letters and sounds.

This is where *phonics* comes in. This method of teaching reading was developed at the end of the nineteenth century. It started with the insight that, before children can learn to read, they need to know how to break a word down into its component sounds. For example, think of all the sounds that occur, almost simultaneously, when you say a one-syllable word like "shrimp," "draft," or "splint." If you have never learned how to read, you do not really analyze those sounds as individual components of a word. You just hear the word as a whole and connect it to its meaning.

Phonics gives children a basic grounding in the different sounds of individual letters. If you were taught phonics at school, you'll remember this process. You learned to sound out each letter on its own, first the "c," then the "a," then the "t." Put it all together and eventually you found yourself saying the word "cat." Pretty soon, you had "a fat cat who sat on a mat, probably thinking about having a rat for lunch." In the phonics textbooks, cats never did anything but sit on mats. This was because phonics grouped together similar-sounding words, so you could learn them all at once and compare them to each other.

Once you'd mastered that step, you could move on to learning how letters sounded in special combinations, like "sh," "th," "ou," or "ai." "The rain in Spain stays mainly on the plain." Finally, you worked up to whole-word recognition, which involved reading words over and over again for practice. "See Jane run. Run, Jane, run." At this point, you also started to learn the words that didn't follow the normal rules of pronunciation. Admittedly, the prose in the Dick and Jane readers had its shortcomings, but, after a few months of this, most children got the hang of reading and moved on to more interesting stories.

Phonics made it possible for you to look at a word you had never seen before and work it out on your own, sounding out the letters, saying them to yourself, until you could make the connection between the written word and the sound of a word you knew.

In about the 1970s, this method fell out of fashion. I'm not an educator, and I don't really know all the ins and outs of the debate, but I gather that phonics, with its drills and repetition, was considered too dull and uncreative. Gradually phonics was abandoned in favor of "whole language." The whole-language approach is based on the assumption that children can learn to read they way they learn to talk—by immersion, without the need for a rigorously structured approach.

Whereas in phonics, the basic unit is an individual letter, in whole language the basic unit is a complete word. Children are given lots of stories with pictures and cartoons that illustrate the words. They are supposed to associate the words with the pictures and the narratives, until gradually they learn what each word looks like. The approach emphasizes the meaning of the words much more than the sound. Children learn words that have unusual pronunciations along with the regular words, but they have to learn each word as a whole. When they come to an unfamiliar word, they can guess what it means from the context, or ignore it and move on.

I'm oversimplifying somewhat. Whole language as an educational philosophy encompasses many other strategies to instill a love of reading in children. Teachers provide children with many different kinds of written materials, not just textbooks and readers, to encourage them to practice their skills. The stories in the readers are also designed to be more interesting and natural-sounding than the stilted artificiality of cats sitting on mats. But the basic approach is to teach children to associate the complete words with their meanings, rather than their sounds.

For some children, this method seems to work reasonably well. Children's brains are quite amazing, and lots of children will learn to read no matter what teaching method is used. But for the 5 to 10 percent of children with dyslexia, the whole-language method does not work at all. It simply does not suit the way their brains function. No matter how gifted and enthusiastic the teacher, no matter how creative and stimulating the reading environment, some children simply do not respond to the whole-language approach. They cannot decode the words on the page. Nothing makes sense. Their marks suffer. They feel frustrated or come to believe they are stupid, because no amount of effort makes the process any easier.

Removing phonics as the mainstay in teaching reading has likely been a factor in what appears to be an increase in reading problems in the past couple of decades. It seems that when all children learned phonics in school, those with mild forms of dyslexia did manage to learn to read, even if they went more slowly than the rest of the class. Their problems never became so acute that they attracted the attention of teachers and parents. With the whole-language approach, however, dyslexic children get left behind completely and their problems are much more noticeable.

The debate over the two approaches to learning reading is becoming heated. Many parents are disappointed by their children's progress with the whole-language method and are demanding back-to-basics education, including phonics. In many areas of North America, a conservative political climate is also favoring a return to more rigorous forms of instruction. I expect the pendulum will probably swing back to phonics in the next few years. In the meantime, however, many dyslexic children are still struggling with a teaching method that doesn't give them the help they need in learning to read.

Alternative theories about dyslexia

As I have explained, the best available research tells us that dyslexia is a specific problem in the brain that affects phonological processing. However, there are many competing theories about the causes of dyslexia. You will probably hear or read about them in popular magazines and see information about them on the Internet, so it's worthwhile to review them here. After all, how you define the problem affects how you treat it. If you think dyslexia is caused by eye problems, for example, you will look for solutions that deal with the eyes.

Serious eye problems do indeed interfere with a child's ability to read, but eye problems are not the same thing as dyslexia. Children who have 20/20 vision may be dyslexic. On the other hand, children who are short-sighted or long-sighted or astigmatic may have no difficulty learning to read. I know an avid reader who has macular degeneration, a very serious eye condition, and is legally blind. Of course, it is possible for a child to have dyslexia and eye problems at the same time, but eye problems do not cause dyslexia.

Most children today have their vision tested before they start school, so that they can be fitted with glasses if they need them. Parents and teachers can easily spot a child with eye problems at an early age. Does he sit very close to the television? Can she identify objects in the distance? Does he notice details in picture books? Does she trip over things that she should be able to see? By the time a child starts to learn to read, any eye problems should have been identified and corrected.

Some optometrists (non-medical professionals who test vision and prescribe glasses) have suggested that "uncoordinated eye movements" cause dyslexia. Researchers have tested this theory by comparing the eye movements of dyslexic and non-dyslexic children. They found no difference whatsoever between the two groups.

A slightly different theory has been advanced by some chiropractors. In 1984, Drs. Carl Ferreri and Richard Wainwright produced a book with the ambitious title *Breakthrough for Dyslexia and Learning Disabilities.* They claimed that learning disabilities are caused by the misalignment of the sphenoid and temporal bones in the skull. This misalignment supposedly interferes with the workings of the nerves leading to the eye muscles. This, in turn, makes eye coordination difficult, which, they believed, caused dyslexia. Researchers have tested this theory by examining the skulls of children with dyslexia and comparing them with the skulls of children who don't have dyslexia. They found no differences. Moreover, Ferreri and Wainwright's theories conflict with much of what is known about the structure of the skull.

In the 1980s, an educational psychologist from California, Helen Irlen, put forward a theory that people with dyslexia have a problem that makes it difficult for their eyes to adapt to light from certain sources, in certain intensities or wavelengths, and to certain forms of color contrast. The ability to adjust to these variations in light is called *scotopic adaptation.* Irlen calls certain forms of dyslexia "scotopic sensitivity syndrome." She received considerable publicity for her ideas when she appeared on the television program "60 Minutes" in 1988. However, there is no reliable research that supports her hypothesis. In fact, it is well known that the part of the eye responsible for reading is quite separate from the part of the eye involved in scotopic adaptation. Nevertheless, the theory persists, along with therapies designed to address "scotopic sensitivity syndrome."

Another group of theories makes a connection between dyslexia and "auditory processing problems." This means the ability to distinguish between similar sounds in spoken words, or to distinguish the details of speech against background noise. A French physician, Alfred Tomatis, has suggested that learning-disabled children lose the ability to listen to certain sounds, and therefore have difficulty understanding what they hear. A similar theory was put forward by another French doctor, Guy Bérard. He suggests that some people hear sounds in unusual ways—either the sounds are distorted, or their hearing of some sounds is too sensitive. He developed a special device called an "audiokinetron" to test hearing and determine the frequencies at which an individual's hearing is too sensitive or not sensitive enough. There is no independently conducted, reliable research that either supports or disproves these theories.

If you are concerned about your child's hearing, you can try some simple tests before you visit a specialist. For example, stand some distance away from your child (at a time when the television is off) and say, "Do you want some ice cream?" in a very quiet voice. Watch the reaction. If your child really does seem to have hearing problems, talk to a specialist. Hearing problems will certainly make it difficult for a child to keep up in school, but there is currently no evidence to suggest that hearing problems are related to dyslexia.

Another theory was put forward in 1972. Jean Ayres, an occupational therapist, suggested that dyslexia is caused by problems in the vestibular system. This is the part of the inner ear that senses the position of the head in relation to gravity (what is up and what is down) and transmits this information to the brain. Children who have problems with their vestibular system have difficulty balancing, for example, when they try to ride a bicycle or use playground equipment. Jean Ayres developed a theory about the relationship of the vestibular system to sight, touch, and the other senses, and suggested that reading problems are caused by poor "sensory integration."

Testing this theory is a straightforward matter. All that is needed is to study a group of children who have dyslexia and compare them with children without dyslexia to see if there are differences in vestibular function that affect balancing. The comparison should be done "blindly"; that is, the observer should not know which group is which. This study was finally done in 1985 by Helene Palatajko, a researcher at the University of Western Ontario, using the best available technology for measuring vestibular function. She found no difference between the two groups. Reading problems and vestibular problems appear to be two quite separate conditions.

Dr. Harold Levinson has suggested a connection between vestibular function, the cerebellum (the part of the brain responsible for coordination), and dyslexia. His theory, put forward in books such as *A Solution to the Riddle Dyslexia*, is related to the fact that certain people cannot read when they are passengers in a moving car, because reading brings on motion sickness. Dr. Levinson suggested that abnormalities of the vestibular system and cerebellum in dyslexic people cause them to experience a form of motion sickness when they try to read. The research that was supposed to support this idea was published in Dr. Levinson's own books, not in refereed medical journals. There is no independent research to support this hypothesis and Dr. Levinson's own research has been criticized by other doctors as inadequate and biased.

A final, unproven theory relating to dyslexia was put forward in the 1960s by Glenn Doman, a physiotherapist, and Carl Delacato, an educator, at the Institute for the Achievement of Human Potential. They suggested that learning problems develop because, for one reason or another, a child does not pass properly through the normal sequence of development in body movement—rolling over, sitting, crawling, standing, walking. They felt that the failure to go through these stages properly indicated problems with the development of the brain and nervous system and eventually led to reading problems. No independent research supports this theory either, and it has been strongly criticized in medical journals.

Not one of these alternative theories about what causes dyslexia is supported by scientific evidence, but they continue to circulate. Wrong-headed ideas never seem to die completely. In fact, the Internet seems to be giving new life to some of them. At the same time, new theories about dyslexia may emerge, because our understanding of the brain is still far from complete. If you hear about a new theory, remember to ask these three questions:

1. What is the evidence that supports this theory? Is it anecdotes from the practice of a particular physician, or does it come from a scientific study?
2. Does the evidence come from an independent source, such as a study at a university or government institution, or is it all coming from the person or group that is putting forward the theory?
3. Is that person or group, in promoting the theory, trying to sell me some expensive therapy or "cure"?

The answers should tell you all you need to know.

Are environmental factors responsible for reading problems?

Pollution in the air, toxic chemicals in household cleaners and paints, additives in food, contaminants in the soil, microorganisms in the water supply, possible radiation from electronic equipment—North Americans often worry about the effects of the environment on health. Could environmental problems play a role in learning disabilities?

The short answer is: Probably not. But let's look at some of the possible culprits and their effects on children. Two environmental factors have been studied for their relationship with learning problems: lead from paint or other sources, and the light and air in classrooms.

Perhaps the most-discussed substance in a child's environment is lead. Lead used to be a component of ordinary house paint. Children who lived in houses where the paint was chipping were at risk of lead poisoning if they frequently swallowed chips of paint. Children were also at risk if they lived near a smelter or near a factory that released lead into the environment, such as companies that made or destroyed car batteries. Houses near highways and busy roads were also likely to be affected by lead from the exhaust of cars that ran on leaded gasoline.

Severe lead poisoning used to be common. Children with lead poisoning—that is, high levels of lead in their bloodstream—suffered from abdominal pain, crankiness, convulsions, anemia, and serious learning problems. Today, however, this severe form of lead poisoning is rare. Lead is no longer added to gasoline or house paint, and new technologies have helped to reduce toxic emissions from factories.

Mild forms of lead poisoning do still occur, however. These do not cause abdominal pain, convulsions, or anemia, but researchers are trying to find out whether or not they would affect a child's ability to concentrate and to learn skills like reading. It is an important area of research, because if there is a link between low levels of lead in the blood and learning disorders, then all children with these problems should be tested for lead in the blood.

At present, there is no consensus. Some experts believe that low blood lead levels are linked to school performance and behavior; others argue that there is no connection.

The reason for the disagreement is that children who are exposed to lead may have other problems that affect their performance at school. For example, a child living in an old house with chipped paint is probably from a poor family. The child may be neglected or may suffer from malnutrition because the parents are struggling to make ends meet. There are many problems that go with being poor, and almost any of them could affect school performance.

Some researchers have shown that exposure to low doses of lead in childhood is related to lower IQ scores, lower ratings from teachers, lower standings in class, and more reading problems. These problems persist even as the children get older. However, other researchers have found that poor performance in school is much more closely related to the parents' IQ and level of education than to lead in the blood.

The question remains: should children with reading and other learning problems be tested routinely for lead in their blood? Most authorities feel that testing is warranted only for children who are at a high risk for lead poisoning—those who live in old houses that have not been painted for many years, or those who live near factories that may release lead into the environment. Otherwise, lead is unlikely to be a factor in a child's learning problems.

What about the classroom environment? Researchers have studied three things in particular: the open-concept classroom, lighting, and air quality.

The open-concept classroom, in which several classes and grades share the same space, concerns some researchers, because they feel it makes it difficult for children to concentrate. There are too many distractions, and the noise level is usually higher than in a small, enclosed classroom. Certainly if a child already has a problem with reading, the open-concept classroom may make things more difficult, but the classroom itself is unlikely to cause the problems.

Other researchers have experimented with different kinds of lighting. In 1976, John Ott, a researcher in Sarasota, Florida, replaced the standard cool-white fluorescent tubes with full-spectrum fluorescent tubes in a windowless classroom. The teachers who participated in this experiment were aware of which kind of lighting was being used at different times. The researcher claimed that the full-spectrum lighting brought about a "dramatic improvement in behavior" in the children with learning and attention problems.

Researchers at the State University of New York at Stony Brook tried the same experiment in 1978, but did not tell the teacher, the children, or the observers which kind of light was being used when. This was done to eliminate any possibility of bias or preference in reporting on the children's behavior. Moreover, these researchers used a different measure of behavior that was more objective and less subject to the personal bias of the observer. They found no difference in the children's behavior when they were exposed to cool-white or full-spectrum fluorescent lighting. It appears that classroom lighting does not affect a child's ability to learn and to read.

Finally, some researchers have experimented with the air quality in classrooms. In 1984, a researcher from the Ontario Institute for Studies in Education tried an experiment with eight children who had learning disabilities, eight children with mild developmental delays, and twenty children who had no learning disabilities. The children were randomly divided into two groups. One group was exposed to ordinary air coming from a fan, and the other to air coming from an ion generator. Then all the children were given memory tests in a laboratory.

The researchers found that all the children who had been exposed to the ion generator did better than the other group.

The theory behind this experiment is that learning-disabled children and children with mild developmental delays have neurotransmitter problems. Neurotransmitters are the chemicals involved in relaying messages between nerve cells in the brain. The negative ions released by the generator were believed to improve the functioning of the neurotransmitters. However, the theory does not explain why the children who didn't have neurotransmitter problems also did better in the memory tests.

The study used only a small number of children, and the memory tests administered in the lab may not be a good substitute for actual classroom performance. Further research in this area is needed to establish whether there is any value in using ion generators in classrooms.

This is not to say that the classroom environment is un-important. All children should be taught in well-lit, well-ventilated spaces. They need the stimulation of having other children around, but they also need time for some peace and quiet, so they can concentrate on their studies. However, at the moment, there is no reliable research that confirms the value of installing special lighting or ion generators in classrooms.

Making the diagnosis of dyslexia

There are two approaches to diagnosing dyslexia. One approach is to administer a series of educational, psychological, medical, and other tests. The other is to use observation, interviews, and common sense. I lean toward the latter view. If the child has dyslexia and no other complicating problems, the diagnosis should be fairly straightforward.

Before you subject your child or a student of yours to a battery of tests, start with what you know already. Consider, for example, a ten-year-old boy I will call John. He's in Grade 5. John was referred to me by his family physician because it appeared that if nothing were done, John would fail his grade. The family doctor had told the family to bring me detailed school reports as well as a record of all the approaches the school authorities had used to try to help John with his learning problems.

When I first met John, I asked him why he had been sent to see me. He looked at the ground, squirmed in his seat a little, and said, "Because I'm not good in school." When I asked him what subjects he was having difficulty with, he said, "Everything." It was clear that he was embarrassed about having to discuss this. I could also tell, when I read his school reports, that John was a bright boy who was having difficulties in those subjects that required reading and writing. He had done quite well up to Grade 3, but was now falling further and further behind.

I pointed out to John that the reports I had received from the school contained evidence that in fact he was a bright boy. He heard this confirmed when I asked the parents about his general development from infancy on. It was clear that he had acquired various skills at the same time as other children his age, and sometimes earlier. For example, he was walking at eleven months, as his mother proudly pointed out. He had been toilet trained at two, and was able to ride a bicycle at five without training wheels. As his parents described these achievements with pride, I could see John was feeling less embarrassed and more relaxed.

I asked John to describe a typical school day for me, subject by subject. It was clear that he did well in art, in music, in physical education, and, until recently, in mathematics. It was also clear that as the requirements for reading and writing had increased in Grade 5, he had fallen behind and was beginning to feel stupid. When I asked his parents how they felt about John's academic progress, it was clear that they were frustrated, because they knew he was bright. When they tried to help him with his homework, it was clear that he had considerable trouble reading.

Both John's parents had done well in school. John's mother was a laboratory technician in a hospital and his father managed a small printing company. Both had attended university and had always hoped that their children would also be able to complete a university degree. However, John's father pointed out that his brother, Allan, had also had significant difficulty with reading and had eventually dropped out of school after Grade 10, having failed several grades. When I asked John's father how Allan was doing now, he told me he was very successful and running a construction company, but that he still did not enjoy reading and never read for pleasure. John's father hoped that I would be able to do something to avoid the stress and strain on the family of Allan's experiences between Grades 5 and 10, and felt that unless something were done, his son would also fail academically as Allan had done.

Both parents pointed out that John had always been quite sociable and friendly, but that over this past school year he had become more withdrawn. Some children were actually picking on him because of his poor school performance. He did not have a behavior problem, but it hurt the parents to see their happy, energetic son becoming shy and withdrawn because of his academic difficulties.

John's school reports revealed that John had begun to have difficulties as early as Grade 1 in reading and writing, but because of his overall intelligence, friendliness, and good discipline in the classroom, his teachers had assumed that he would outgrow the problem. By Grade 3 the problems were getting worse and, since John was having some difficulty concentrating in classes that required reading or writing, the teacher began to wonder if the main problem might not be behavioral, such as a lack of motivation. John was receiving more and more reprimands from the teacher. The teachers sent notes to John's home more and more frequently to tell the parents that John wasn't paying attention in the classroom and wasn't completing his work.

The teacher had met with John's parents to discuss the problem. Together, they decided that John should see the school psychologist. The psychologist administered a number of tests that confirmed that John was intelligent. He suggested that John remain in the regular classroom for most of the school day but that he have extra help several times a week in a special small-group setting to work on the subjects in which he was having the most difficulty. John had had this extra coaching all the way through Grade 4, but his progress in reading and writing was minimal.

I asked John and his parents what effect John's school difficulties were having on family life. It was clear that both parents were motivated to help John and had often worked with him after school to help him finish his assignments, but they were becoming frustrated with the amount of time it took John to complete his work. John's younger brother Timothy, an eight-year-old in Grade 3 and an excellent student, was beginning to resent the amount of time his parents spent helping John with his studies at home. Although his parents tried not to compare John's scholastic ability with that of his brother Timothy, it was clear that John dreaded report-card day when his parents would praise Timothy for his excellent schoolwork but could not do the same for him.

During the course of my interview with John and his parents, the parents raised the question of attention deficit hyperactivity disorder (ADHD). They had heard that children with this disorder also could not complete assignments, and also did not progress academically as well as their potential should have allowed them to do. They pointed out that the teachers had told them that John was inattentive during much of the class time and they had heard that this was a key component of the diagnosis of ADHD.

I asked them about John's attention span for things he enjoyed, such as drawing or building Lego constructions or doing jigsaw puzzles. They said that he could spend at least an hour of unsupervised time doing these activities without getting up once. In reviewing the school report, I noticed that the art teacher and the music teacher made no comments about inattentiveness and clearly considered John to be doing very well in those subjects. The problem with inattention occurred only in subjects that called for reading or writing.

At this point I asked John to do some reading for me. He was about two grade levels behind where he should be. I gave John a written math problem to look at. He had difficulty with it, but when I read the problem out to him, he solved it immediately.

By this point in the interview, it was clear that John's major problem was dyslexia. Clearly, John's uncle Allan also had dyslexia. I told the family that this was an inherited condition. I also told John that dyslexia had nothing to do with intelligence, and that many people with this problem were able to go on to university and have successful careers. I reminded him that his uncle, who had had similar reading problems, was a very successful businessman.

I did not recommend any further testing for John. I told the family that phonics remediation had been proven to be successful for children like John and that I would get in touch with John's teacher and make a strong recommendation that John be started on phonics remediation. I suggested that the parents meet with the teacher and work with John at home so that both at home and at school John would get help with phonics and that his reading would be made substantially better.

This interview is typical of hundreds I have done with children and their parents. These are the basic steps:

1. I talk to the child and gather impressions about his or her intelligence and personality. I ask the child to describe a typical day at school. Children are often shy with doctors and embarrassed about their problems, but it's important to make them part of the interview and not just talk over their heads with the parents.

2. I eliminate the possibility that the child has a developmental delay of some kind that would affect school performance by asking the parents questions about the child's early childhood. When did the child learn to sit up, crawl, walk, complete toilet training, feed himself, dress herself? Although different children learn these things at different times, if the child is very late in learning all or most of these things, it may suggest a developmental disorder.

3. I test the child's reading ability. This gives me an idea of the severity of the problem. John was reading at a Grade 3 level in Grade 5. Some children may be reading at a Grade 1 or 2 level in Grade 5, which suggests that they have a more serious problem than John.

4. I give the child a written math problem to solve. If the child is clearly having difficulty, I read it aloud. If the child can solve it at that point, it confirms that the problem is with reading itself, not with the content of written material.

5. I look at report cards, which give me a sense of when the child started to have difficulty in school. The pattern is usually the same: when any subject starts to involve individual reading rather than group discussions and other activities, the child starts to fall behind the rest of the class. The report cards and school comments are also a good indication of whether the child is intelligent.

6. I try to find out if there is a history of dyslexia or other learning problems in the family.

7. I ask about the child's capacity for paying attention to activities that he or she enjoys, such as hobbies, arts and crafts, and board games. If the child is able to pay attention for extended periods to activities that don't involve reading and writing but that do involve concentration, ADHD is *unlikely to be a factor*.

This approach is based on the best available research about dyslexia. Unless there are complicating factors in the diagnosis, there is no need to subject a child to a battery of tests, which can be stressful for the child (the very word "battery" suggests the effect on a child), not to mention time-consuming, and, in some cases, expensive for the parents.

Nevertheless, I will describe some of the other tests that may be suggested to you, so you can make up your mind how much testing is appropriate for your child.

IQ tests

Many school boards, but not all, require a child to take an IQ test before the board will permit a child with reading or other learning problems to get special help.

IQ tests can be useful up to a point, but you shouldn't put too much faith in them. Intelligence is a notoriously slippery thing to define, let alone measure. The idea that the complex workings of a person's mind can be summed up in a single number is, when you think about it, absurd. Nevertheless, IQ tests have been used and misused for years, to rank children and adults, and sometimes to justify eugenics programs or restrictive immigration policies. The tests are full of flaws, such as cultural bias. Doctors, parents, and educators need to keep them in perspective.

It may help to know that, strictly speaking, the tests do not measure "intelligence" at all, only the ability to keep up in school. The original IQ tests were designed in the early twentieth century as a way to predict academic achievement and to identify children in need of special education. The first tests were developed by a French psychologist called Alfred Binet. He came up with a test made up of hundreds of questions, selected more or less at random. Binet administered this test to thousands of schoolchildren and compared the test results with the children's school reports. If children who were doing well in school tended to do well on certain questions, and children who were doing poorly in school tended to get the same questions wrong, he kept those questions in the test. He deleted questions that did not tend to mirror the performance of the children in their schoolwork. In this way, Binet created a final test that would be a fairly reliable predictor of how children would do in school.

The tests have been translated, revised, modernized, and revamped since then. Today's tests are marked out of 200 and the average score range is 85–115. Children with scores below this range tend to do poorly in school, and those who get scores above this range tend to do better than average.

There is no single form of the test; many different IQ tests exist. One contemporary IQ test is based on Binet's original test. It's called the "Stanford–Binet Test," and it can be used for children of two years of age up to the late teens. Some of the questions have been updated, some are much the same as the original questions thought up nearly 100 years ago. The test has fifteen subtests in four areas: verbal reasoning, quantitative reasoning, abstract and visual reasoning, and short-term memory.

The other commonly used test is the "Wechsler Intelligence Scale for Children—Revised" (WISC-R). This is usually administered to children between the ages of six and sixteen. There are ten or twelve subtests. Half of them measure verbal ability, and half measure non-verbal or "performance" ability. The verbal tests deal with information, similarities, arithmetic, vocabulary, and comprehension. The non-verbal tests require children to complete pictures, arrange images to form a story, put together blocks in a prescribed pattern, assemble puzzles, work through mazes, and so forth.

Most psychologists feel that these two are the most reliable IQ tests available, although other forms exist.

The main reason for using these tests is to rule out the possibility that a child who is experiencing difficulty in reading has some form of general neurological or developmental problem. A child who is neurologically impaired or developmentally delayed will have difficulty with all the tasks in these tests. However, if the child simply has a reading problem, he or she should get an average or above-average score.

Perhaps another function of IQ tests is simply to reassure the parents and the child that having reading problems does not mean that one is "stupid." Parents and teachers know from observation when a child is intelligent, but it may help to reinforce this intuitive knowledge with a supposedly objective measurement.

There is no other reason to give a child an IQ test. The test provides no insight into the nature or severity of the particular problem. In fact, researchers have found that IQ scores tell us little or nothing about a child's reading skills. In a 1988 study done by Linda Siegel of the Ontario Institute for Studies in Education, reading-disabled and non-reading-disabled children between the ages of seven and sixteen were divided into four groups, according to their IQ scores. They were then given tests of reading, spelling, language, math, and memory. Siegel found that reading-disabled children did poorly on all the tests, compared with the other children, no matter what their IQ scores were. At the same time, however, some children with low IQ scores were found to be good readers. Siegel argues that IQ scores are irrelevant in defining and diagnosing learning disorders and she has widespread support for her position.

In some cases, the test can produce unreliable results. Bright children suffering from ADHD may do poorly on the tests because they find it hard to focus, but this doesn't mean they are of subnormal intelligence. There is also nothing to suggest that children who have learning problems benefit in the long run from having taken a test. The research in this area just hasn't been done.

Tests of academic ability

There are many tests of academic ability that are routinely administered in schools. Indeed, standardized testing is something of a growth industry at the moment. In Ontario, where I live, province-wide testing in Grade 3 has been established, and, across North America, standardized testing is increasing, ostensibly to increase the "accountability" of schools. These tests are controversial and have been criticized by academics as being unrelated to the core curriculum. The important thing to remember is that, in state-wide or province-wide tests, your child's individual score cannot be interpreted, except in relation to the scores of other children in the same classroom. In a sense, these tests are evaluating the schools and the teachers, not the students. Unlike the IQ tests, there is no clear "average" range of scores.

There are, however, tests of academic achievement that are a more reliable guide to the grade level at which a child is performing. Two are considered especially reliable.

- The "Metropolitan Achievement Test" is a group test for children from kindergarten through Grade 12 that measures achievement in language, reading, mathematics, science, and social studies. It is administered in the classroom, so it shows how children perform in classroom conditions.
- The "Wide Range Achievement Test" focuses on reading, spelling, and arithmetic. There are two levels, one used for children five to eleven, and the other for children over eleven. The test is administered individually and includes word recognition, dictation, counting, number recognition, and oral problems. It also has a good reputation as a valid test of children's achievement.

These tests provide only a final score. The results do not normally include an analysis of why a child made certain kinds of errors. For example, one child might spell a word incorrectly but phonetically, while another spells the same word incorrectly in a way that shows an inability to connect letters and sounds, which might indicate dyslexia. The children are wrong for different reasons, but the final scores of both children show only that a mark was deducted for the wrong answer. Unless a skilled evaluator goes over the individual test results carefully to determine why a child gave an incorrect answer, these distinctions will not be picked up.

Medical tests

Most schoolchildren are routinely tested for vision problems, either by their doctor or a public health nurse. If the child has not been tested recently, a simple, rapid test can be conducted in a doctor's office to make sure that the child's vision has not deteriorated since the last test.

There is no need to test for uncoordinated eye movements, "scotopic sensitivity," or abnormal placement of bones in the head, since these tests are based on theories about the causes of dyslexia that have been shown to be incorrect. Similarly, you do not need to have the child tested for "visual perceptual skills." Occupational therapists may sometimes recommend this test, which is intended to identify people who have difficulty with such things as distinguishing left and right, reading maps, following directions, and finding objects around the house. Although dyslexic (and non-dyslexic) people may have these problems, the tests available are too unreliable to be useful. A child who is tested twice or more may get very different scores each time.

Hearing tests are probably not necessary. Children who have significant problems with hearing will also have problems with pronouncing words. Their families will notice that they can't hear certain voices and sounds. If the family is in any doubt, a simple test can be administered by the child's doctor. Tests of "auditory processing," however, have been shown to be of no value whatsoever.

Tests of the vestibular system or cerebellum, which affect motor function and coordination, are not useful. The study, conducted in 1985 by Helene Polatajko, involved examining a large group of children with reading and other learning problems and another large group of children similar in all respects except for the fact that they did not have learning problems. The lab technicians who tested the children for motor function and coordination were not told which children had learning problems. It turned out that there was no relation between learning problems and motor function and coordination.

No special neurological tests, such as the electroencephalograph (EEG), which tests brain-wave functioning, or magnetic resonance imaging (MRI), which shows the structure of the brain, are needed. Researchers investigating learning disorders use these tests to learn more about the ways in which the brains of people with dyslexia differ from other people's brains, but there is no value in subjecting an average child with reading or other learning problems to these tests. They can be quite stressful for the child, and they serve no useful purpose in individual diagnosis.

You can also rule out most blood tests (which most children hate anyway). If you live in an old house with old paint on the walls, or near a factory that may be releasing lead into the environment, you might want to test the child's blood lead levels. Otherwise, this test is unnecessary. You also don't need to have the child's chromosomes analyzed. If the child has a chromosomal problem that is causing developmental delays, such as Down's syndrome, the condition will be identified long before the child is old enough to go to school.

Your doctor may recommend a blood thyroid-hormone test if there is reason to believe that the child has an overactive or underactive thyroid gland. If the gland is overactive (hyperthyroidism) the child will be very fidgety and often sweaty. She will feel hot when everyone else is cool and her eyes may have a staring, slightly "buggy" appearance. If the gland is underactive (hypothyroidism), the child will be sluggish and may suffer from chronic constipation. His growth and general development will be slower than that of other children. In either case, the symptoms of thyroid dysfunction are often more noticeable and worrisome than any learning problems, and the doctor will recommend blood tests to check thyroid function.

No other blood tests are needed. You may read about tests for trace elements. These are minerals and other chemicals found in minute amounts in the body. Health-food promoters have suggested that deficiencies of minerals such as copper, zinc, magnesium, manganese, and chromium lead to learning problems. There is no research to support this hypothesis, and no need to test children's blood for these minerals. As you might expect, the only people who recommend blood tests for trace elements are the people who sell mineral supplements.

Likewise, blood sugar levels have no bearing on dyslexia. Low blood sugar (hypoglycemia) may cause dizziness, headaches, sweating, hunger, blurred vision, and even convulsions. Many popular books have been published about the "evils" of sugar, blaming refined sugar and junk food for many different health problems. However, sugar consumption is unrelated to dyslexia.

Not all reading difficulties indicate dyslexia

Sometimes doctors and teachers are a little too quick to put a label on a child who is having problems at school. Not all reading problems are caused by learning disorders. Learning to read is a difficult skill, and dyslexia is not the only reason why a child might fall behind. Be very careful not to jump to conclusions. To give you an example, I will describe another child I was once asked to see.

Hector was an eleven-year-old boy who had come with his mother from Colombia four years before I met him. He was in Grade 5, and he had already failed one grade. Hector was referred to me by his family physician, who felt that Hector was in danger of being failed again and who wondered if Hector might have a specific learning disorder such as dyslexia.

When I saw Hector and his mother, it was clear that, although Hector spoke reasonable English, his mother spoke only Spanish. When I reviewed his report cards, I could see that Hector was having problems in most of his academic subjects, except in areas that did not require reading, writing, or mathematics. For example, he did well in music, art, and physical education. There was no evidence that he was a behavior problem in the classroom, and he appeared to have no difficulty making friends with other children.

Hector told me that he had taken English as a second language when he first came from Colombia and felt pretty comfortable speaking English, but that he found his academic subjects quite hard. I tested Hector's reading. It was at least two grade levels behind where it should have been. I also gave him some relatively simple math problems to solve. When he had trouble reading them, I read them out to him. He still had difficulty determining whether he had to multiply, add, subtract, or divide.

With the help of an interpreter, I was able to find out from his mother that Hector's development had been entirely normal. He had learned to walk, talk, feed himself, and dress himself at the usual ages, and toilet training had not been a particular problem. It was also clear that Hector's mother had no difficulty with his behavior at home, nor were there any difficulties in the neighborhood. I asked her whether other members of her family had difficulty reading. Since not all of her relatives had completed school, it was hard to be sure, but she didn't seem to think that reading was a particular problem in her family.

I asked Hector how he spent his time when he came home from school. He told me that he usually watched television. When he came home in the afternoon, his mother was usually out working as a house cleaner. When they finished dinner, he and his mother usually watched television until bedtime. Hector also told me that most of his friends in the neighborhood were also from Spanish-speaking countries. Most of them spoke Spanish when they played together.

The interview did not give me any reason to believe that Hector had dyslexia, even though he had trouble reading. He was a perfectly normal, healthy boy who apparently lacked motivation to learn his academic subjects. He wasn't doing his homework most evenings and had therefore fallen behind his classmates. Because he had been failed once already, he believed that his abilities were limited. His mother did not encourage or pressure him to improve his grades. She was so busy trying to make ends meet that, as long as Hector was staying out of trouble, she was content.

I felt that it would be a mistake to fail Hector a second time; it would only confirm his low self-esteem. However, I also felt that he should not be promoted without some intervention by the school board. I talked to the principal and suggested that Hector be given as much extra help as possible, on a one-to-one basis, in a resource room with a specially trained teacher who could motivate him, at the same time working on his specific deficiencies, such as reading, writing, and mathematics. I also felt it was important for the school to have an interpreter talk to Hector's mother so that, in the evenings, instead of simply letting him watch television, she could monitor his homework and ensure that it was done.

Six months after I initially saw Hector, I saw him again and was pleased to learn that his performance in school had improved at least one grade level. The principal was so encouraged by his improvement that he was going to allow Hector to work with the resource-room teacher for the rest of the school year.

Hector is a good example of a child who has trouble reading for reasons that have nothing to do with dyslexia. He needed a little pushing to do better in school. He needed to spend more time on his homework. He didn't need a label that didn't fit him.

What do we do now? How to help a child with a reading disability

The simplest, most effective way to help dyslexic children learn to read is to teach them reading using the phonics method. Ideally, children will study phonics in school with a teacher, and also spend some time practicing phonics at home with their parents.

The evidence that this approach is the most effective one for dyslexia comes from studies such as that done in 1983 by Drs. Rachel Gittelman and Ingrid Feingold at Columbia University in New York and published in the *Journal of Child Psychology and Psychiatry*. I want to describe the research in detail, because you may need to describe it to school authorities yourself to explain why you think a child should be enrolled in a phonics program.

Gittelman and Feingold conducted a randomized controlled trial of reading remediation programs for children with reading difficulties. All the children selected for the trial were of average intelligence; had no visual, behavioral, or attentional problems; and came from stable families. However, they all had problems with reading, and there was a noticeable difference between their grade level and their reading ability.

The children were randomly assigned to two groups. The two groups were compared to make sure that they were similar in terms of average age; the proportion of boys and girls; and the proportions of children of different races, social classes, and religions. The reading problems in both groups were also similar. This comparison was done to make sure that any changes that occurred over the course of the study would be a result of the treatment itself and not other factors.

One group was given a four-month reading remediation program that heavily emphasized phonics. Whole-word recognition was introduced, but mostly the children studied phonics. The other group received tutoring for four months in other subjects, but no phonics instruction. This tutoring was intended to be an "attention placebo." The researchers wanted to make sure that any improvements in the reading remediation group were the result of the kind of tutoring they were getting, not just the fact that they were receiving extra attention.

At the end of the four months, all the children were given a standard test of reading ability. The group that had studied phonics had improved remarkably. Most had improved their reading by a full grade. The children in the attention placebo group had improved very little, if at all. The test was repeated eight months later. The children from the reading remediation group were still doing better than those in the other group. However, because they had received no further instruction, they were still behind in reading, compared with children without reading problems.

Gittelman and Feingold came to the following conclusions:

- Reading intervention in the form of phonics really does help children with reading problems.
- Four months isn't long enough to overcome their reading problems completely.
- The improvement does, however, last even after the treatment.
- A battery of tests to identify specific types of reading problems is unnecessary; no tests were done, but all the children in the reading remediation group improved.

I consider this research a model of its kind, and I am surprised that it is not more widely known. Only now that laboratory research is confirming that dyslexia is a problem of phonological processing are educators beginning to accept that phonics is the best way to help children with dyslexia. Still, many do not know about this research and are not convinced of the value of phonics. If you are a parent, you may have to persuade the teacher at your child's school to teach your child phonics. If you are a teacher, you may have to persuade the school principal to let you teach phonics to children with reading problems.

As class sizes get larger and school budgets get smaller, it may be hard to get a child into a reading remediation program. Most schools require a battery of tests before a child is admitted into any special program, and the special program may not include phonics. Parents may find themselves on their own, coping with a child's reading problems.

How parents can help a child with reading

If your child has dyslexia and special help at school is not available, don't give up. You can teach your child phonics yourself. All it takes is a commitment of your time and attention.

You can buy a phonics instruction book at the bookstore, or get educational software that uses phonics, but you don't need to spend a lot of money. If you cannot afford these options, use the resources at your library. Your child's teacher or a children's librarian can recommend a book to start with. You can even create your own methods. All that is required is to help the child learn to sound out letters individually and in different combinations. If you can read, you can do that. Even an older sibling may be able to help out on occasion. The Somalian father I mentioned earlier simply spent evening after evening helping his son sound out the words in his schoolbooks.

Here are a few ideas for helping your child with phonics and reading:

- Try to set aside time every day for reading.
- Postpone the session if the child is too tired, hungry, or cranky to pay attention.
- Don't overdo it at first: start with ten or fifteen minutes a day.
- Set achievable goals: a page a day of a phonics book or a reader may be enough at first.
- Be positive and praise your child when she reads correctly. When she makes mistakes, be patient and help correct the error. If she hesitates, allow time before you rush in to help.
- When you read a story together, make sure that the child not only sounds out the words, but makes sense of them too. Ask him what he thinks of the story or the characters.
- Start by reading the first few pages or paragraphs of a story aloud to get the child hooked. Then ask the child to read the rest of the story to find out what happens next.
- Vary the activity by spending some sessions doing word games instead of reading. Or ask the child to make up a story, write it down for her, and get her to read it back to you.
- Don't make these sessions a substitute for reading aloud to your child. If you've always read him a bedtime story, keep it up. It will help him associate books with enjoyment.
- Reward her when she does especially well or when you see a real improvement in her school marks.

You have to be prepared for an investment of time. It may take months, or even years, until the child is reading at the appropriate grade level. However, phonics does work, and that time will pay off in the child's improved performance and self-esteem.

How schools respond to learning problems

Different schools take different approaches to helping children who need extra help. Some schools offer full-time special-education classes, either for children with specific problems such as reading, or for children who are falling behind in all subjects.

Another approach is to set up a resource room where children can receive extra help in a small class with a specially trained teacher. A child may take these classes for one period a day or for half a day every day, and spend the rest of the time in regular classes.

A third approach is called "mainstreaming." The child stays in the regular classroom all day, but an education specialist is available to provide support to the teacher and to spend some time individually with the child, working on reading problems.

Finally, some schools advocate "retention," which is the politically correct term for failing the child and making him or her repeat a year, in the belief that exposing the child to the same material all over again will improve the child's performance.

A school's choice of one or other of these approaches is usually based on its budget, staffing, and resources, and not on evidence that one approach is more effective than any other. The truth is, the research just hasn't been done to find out if one method works better than another. A few studies have compared full-time special-education classes to mainstreaming, but they were not randomized controlled trials. Some appeared to show that children who remained in their regular classes did better, but this may have been because children with more severe problems were selected for the special-education classes. There is also no proof that retention makes much difference in a child's academic performance, and every likelihood that it damages the child's self-esteem. On the other hand, "social promotion," which means letting children with learning problems move up from grade to grade with their peers, even though they have not had remedial help and their academic performance has not improved, doesn't help either. The children know that they are falling farther and farther behind, and they may come to believe they are stupid. Even putting a child in a special-education class may make a child feel singled out.

Based on the available evidence, the best approach seems to be to have the child's regular classroom teacher, with support from a specialist, if necessary, provide reading remediation in the form of phonics. If this is not possible, giving the child help in a resource room is probably the best alternative.

How teachers can help a child who has reading problems

Some of the teachers I have talked to say that they don't feel they have the training to deal with learning-disabled children. They have never had to teach phonics and feel ill-equipped to offer effective reading remediation. However, as school budgets shrink and special-education classes with them, more and more teachers will have learning-disabled children in their regular classrooms.

Although some teachers may need extra training or support, most teachers can learn to accommodate dyslexic children in the classroom. Once you understand what dyslexia means and how children experience it, you can easily think of ways to help. For example, when you hand out written instructions for an assignment, you can read them over to the class, to ensure that everyone knows what is expected, or you can allow a non-dyslexic student to read them aloud quietly to a dyslexic student. You can tape material for dyslexic students to listen to at home and allow them to take certain tests orally. Make sure that they have extra time to complete written work in class or to read an assigned passage from a textbook. Avoid asking dyslexic students to read aloud in class.

If you need to provide reading remediation, you should consult with a reading specialist on appropriate materials. For example, if you are teaching a twelve-year-old who is reading at a Grade 4 level, he or she will not find Grade 4 texts very interesting. You will need to find special materials written in simple language on topics of interest to twelve-year-olds. Fortunately, more and more of these kinds of materials are now available. Some are used in adult-literacy or English as a Second Language (ESL) classes.

Reading remediation for dyslexic students is largely a matter of helping them connect the sound of words to their written form. You will need to spend time with the student. You cannot just hand out a workbook and expect the student to work through it without supervision. Sometimes you may want students to work on lists of individual words in isolation, but most of the time they need to read stories and articles that put words in context. Keep the activities varied, and encourage students to listen to, say, and write words as well as reading them silently.

Some schools recommend "strategies training" for reading problems. This approach is not particularly useful for children with dyslexia, but it can help students who are able to read but unable to remember what they have read as they go along. These children are taught to pause every few sentences and picture in their minds what they have just read. Studies on strategies training show that it helps children who have difficulty organizing information in their minds and recalling it later, but it doesn't make much difference if the child cannot easily read the information in the first place.

What about computer-assisted learning?

In some cases, children may be able to use phonics software programs on computers in school. More and more schools are installing computers, and a number of programs offer phonics instruction. One study of these programs, conducted by researchers at Florida State University in 1987, divided a group of children with reading problems into two. One half spent fifteen minutes a day, five days a week, working with a program called "I Iint and Hunt" that included audio, and gave the sound of each letter as it appeared on the screen. It was a game-like program that the children enjoyed playing. The other half of the group did spelling drills on the computer. At the end of several weeks, the group that had worked with the phonics software had improved their reading skills.

In a 1994 study, Barbara Wise and Richard Olson at the University of Colorado compared computer reading programs to regular language-arts instruction. They divided a group of children with reading problems into two groups. Half the children spent thirty minutes a day, three or four days a week, using "talking" computers that read out stories as the words appeared on the screen. The other half spent the time in a regular language-arts class that did not involve phonics. At the end of the study, the two groups were tested for word recognition. The group that had used computers did better on these tests than the other group.

All these studies tell us is that, when children with reading problems get a chance to practice phonics, whether in a regular classroom or on a computer, their reading skills improve. This provides more evidence for the importance of phonics, but it doesn't tell us much about the value of computers as teaching aids.

One advantage of computers is that most children enjoy using them. Children can make mistakes on a computer and correct those mistakes in private, rather than in front of others in a classroom. Also, the feedback from computers is immediate and consistent. This means that they are useful for drills and for helping children practice the skills they have already acquired.

Computers may not be as effective, however, in introducing new skills. Much depends on the design and quality of the software or CD-ROM, which can vary widely. Many programs and hypermedia texts provide more opportunities for play than for real learning. A routine complaint about computers in the schools is that children who are spending time in front of a screen, using a mouse to point at and click on the words and images, are not really learning useful skills. For a child who finds reading difficult, the temptation to play on the computer, rather than practice reading skills, may be particularly strong.

Computers can supplement reading remediation classes or tutoring, but they are no substitute for help from teachers and parents.

The role of psychological intervention: relaxation, hypnosis, and psychotherapy

Psychologists have proposed a number of therapies to help children who have reading problems. These include relaxation therapy, with or without biofeedback; hypnosis; and psychotherapy.

Relaxation therapy is based on the assumption that stress or fear can prevent a child from learning to read. Teaching the child how to relax in the classroom when a difficult subject is being taught will enable him or her to learn more and do better work.

One study, conducted in Texas by John Carter and Harold Russell, tested this idea using biofeedback as an indicator of states of relaxation. In biofeedback, wires are taped to the skin to record body temperature and muscle tension. People who are relaxed tend to have slightly higher body temperatures and more relaxed muscles. If the biofeedback shows that someone is not relaxed, then he or she is instructed to consciously relax and pay attention to the measurements of the biofeedback system. People can try different relaxation methods and see which one makes the most difference to the measurements.

The study divided young boys with similar learning problems into two groups. One group received ten biofeedback sessions over a five-week period. The boys in this group also practiced relaxation at home three times a week, using a prerecorded audiotape. The tape contained instructions on relaxing the muscles and thinking relaxing thoughts. (In a later phase of the study, children whose parents could not afford tape recorders did this part of the therapy at school.) The other group, which was the control group, received no special treatment at all. In other words, in this experiment, there was no attention placebo group.

When the experiment was over, the boys in the relaxation therapy/biofeedback group did better on tests of reading and handwriting than the boys in the control group. However, since there was no attention placebo group, it is impossible to say whether this change came about simply because they were the object of special attention and they believed that the therapies were working. Also the tests were only done once, on the day after the treatment was completed, so there is no way of knowing whether the improvements were lasting.

Another study, carried out by researchers in Calgary, worked with children who tended to be impulsive and inattentive in class. These children were divided into three groups. One group listened to relaxation audiotapes while lying back in a reclining chair. The second group were taught self-instructional relaxation techniques, such as repeating to themselves, "If I go slowly and carefully, I can do a good job." The audiotape and self-instruction sessions lasted thirty minutes and were repeated ten times over four weeks. The control group had no special activities. All three groups given tests of impulsiveness and attention in a laboratory before and after the study.

The results were unclear. The group that used audiotapes did no better than the self-instruction group, and although both were better than the control group in some tests, in other tests, the control group did better. It might have been more helpful to have tested the children in the real-world classroom setting, rather than using lab tests.

At present, there is no very good evidence for the usefulness of relaxation therapy for children with learning or reading problems. Biofeedback may help in the short term, but the improvement may simply be a placebo effect. Nor does relaxation therapy appear to help children with problems of inattention or impulsive behavior.

As for hypnosis, the evidence is equally unclear. Tests have been done, but so far, all of them have been poorly designed. Only a few children have been studied, the children are not randomly allocated to treatment and control groups, researchers and participants are not "blinded" (that is, they know which group is which and this knowledge may color their judgment), and there has been no followup to find out if any improvements are long-lasting. At this point, I cannot recommend hypnosis, because there is no evidence that it does much good or that it does more good than harm.

Finally, some psychologists may suggest psychotherapy, either for the child alone, or for the child and the family together, or for a group of similar children.

The use of individual psychotherapy is based on the assumption that a child with a reading or learning problem may have an unconscious need not to do well in school. By performing poorly, the child may get more attention from the family or the teacher. The therapist talks to the child to find out why he or she feels that academic success would be a disadvantage and to help the child understand that he or she has more to gain from doing well.

Family psychotherapy starts from the assumption that the child's problems are rooted in family conflicts, and that, when these are resolved, the child will do better in school. The therapist works with the whole family to uncover the sources of conflict and to help family members sort out their problems and live together more amicably.

In group therapy, the child is encouraged to discuss problems at home or at school in a group with other children. The group is facilitated by a therapist. Group members provide peer support and feedback, and help the child understand that he or she is not alone in dealing with problems.

All these methods were developed before scientists discovered that the main cause of learning problems was a genetic problem in the brain, not a problem that developed after a child was born. Psychotherapy can help children with problems in their relationships with parents or teachers or other children. It can also help children recover from a psychologically traumatic event in their lives. What it can't do is make a difference to an inherited disorder such as dyslexia, any more than it could make a difference to a condition like diabetes. Not surprisingly, therefore, there is no definitive research that shows that psychotherapy helps dyslexic children improve their reading skills.

That doesn't mean that psychologists and counselors don't have a role to play in helping children with reading problems. If the child's reading problems have caused family conflict, or if the child feels socially isolated because of reading problems and has difficulty establishing friendly relationships with other children, psychotherapy can help. But psychotherapy should never take the place of intensive reading remediation using phonics. Once the child's reading problems start to improve, psychotherapy can help with the problems that accompany dyslexia. But if the reading problems remain untreated, there is little point in a course of psychotherapy.

The unproven therapies

Just as there are many unscientific theories about what causes dyslexia, there are some unscientific methods of treating the problem. You will probably see them mentioned in advertisements or on the Internet, so you should know a little about them.

Vision training programs

These programs involve eye exercises and sometimes body exercises, such as the use of balance beams. Studies of these programs show some interesting results:

- Vision training does improve eye movements.
- Studies that use a placebo attention group show that that group does just as well as the treatment group; therefore, the improvement is due to the attention, not the eye exercises.

Since problems with eye coordination have nothing to do with dyslexia, improving eye coordination won't improve reading ability. However, giving children extra attention, whatever form that attention may take, does seem to help with school performance. Most parents and teachers would consider this finding self-evident, but it's always nice to see it confirmed in the research.

Tinted (Irlen) lenses

Irlen lenses are sold through franchises and also on the Internet. They are expensive, more than $500 (U.S.) for a set. It worries me to see parents pay such large sums of money for treatments that are known to be ineffective. Indeed, several studies, many of which have been published in the *Journal of Learning Disabilities*, have shown conclusively that Irlen lenses do not improve the reading ability of dyslexic children. Naturally, everyone would like a quick way to solve the problem of dyslexia, but this isn't it.

The American Academy of Pediatrics, the American Association of Pediatric Ophthalmology and Strabismus, and the American Academy of Ophthalmology have issued a joint statement to say that reading disabilities should be treated only with methods that have been proven to be effective and that Irlen lenses and eye exercises have not been proven effective. The statement reads, in part: "Individuals who have learning disabilities should . . . avoid remedies involving eye exercises, filters, tinted lenses, or other optical devices that have no known scientific proof of efficacy."

Auditory processing

There are two forms of auditory-processing training. The first, called "Listening Training," or sometimes, redundantly, "Auditory Listening Training," was developed in the 1950s by a French doctor, Alfred Tomatis. Tomatis believed that some children lost the ability to listen to certain sounds, which makes it difficult for them to understand what they hear. This inability is said to lead to a number of learning and behavioral problems, including autism, attention deficit hyperactivity disorder, dyslexia, depression, and stuttering.

Tomatis's therapy involves listening to music (usually Mozart or Gregorian chant) and other sounds (including tapes of the child's mother's voice) through special headphones. The music is modified at first to remove all sounds below a certain frequency. The intent is to "strengthen" the ear by repeating certain frequencies over and over until the individual can hear them clearly. The therapy was publicized in the book *The Mozart Effect* by Don Campbell. The director of the Toronto Tomatis Centre, Paul Madaule, has also written a book called *When Listening Comes Alive,* in which he claims that the Tomatis method helped him overcome dyslexia.

The second therapy is called "Auditory Integration Training" (AIT). It was developed by Guy Bérard, who had used the Tomatis method to treat his own hearing problems. Bérard developed a theory that some people hear sounds in an unusual way, either because their hearing is insufficiently sensitive and distorts sounds, or because their hearing is exceptionally sensitive and certain sounds are too painful to experience.

AIT starts with a test of hearing using a device called an "audiokinetron" that is intended to determine which sounds are distorted or painful and whether the problem is one of undersensitivity or oversensitivity. Then the person is required to listen to music that does not contain the particular frequencies that are difficult to listen to. The idea is that the hearing needs to "rest" and recuperate from certain sounds in order to heal itself. Once healed, the ear will be able to hear better, and learning will be improved. This is more or less the opposite approach to that used in Tomatis's Listening Training.

Like the Tomatis method, AIT is credited with the ability to help children suffering from a variety of learning and behavioral problems. It was widely publicized in a book about an autistic child called *The Sound of a Miracle* by Annabel Stehli.

Both kinds of training can be very expensive and usually require many visits to a special training center. Unfortunately, there is no reliable evidence that either program has any effect on learning difficulties. Even the Web site for one of the training centers admits that there is very little documentation on the actual effects of the training. Until an independent researcher conducts a proper randomized controlled trial to test these therapies, there is no reason to believe that they are effective, and every reason not to spend money on them when more effective and less expensive treatments are available.

Sensory integration therapies

These therapies are designed for children who have problems with balancing and coordination. Their use in treating children with learning disabilities originated with the theories of Jean Ayres, which I describe on pages 40–41. The therapies use equipment such as scooters, swings, or chairs that spin around.

These therapies have been tested in randomized controlled trials, which have shown that they make no difference whatsoever to academic abilities, although they may help children who have problems balancing. One particular study, conducted in 1984, put children in three groups. One was a control group and received no therapy; the second group received sensory integration therapy, and the third group received perceptual motor therapy. (Perceptual motor therapy is an occupational therapy designed to help a child with fine motor skills such as holding a pencil, cutting and pasting, or tracing, and gross motor skills such as skipping, hopping, or jumping.) Although the children in the two groups who received therapy did improve on tests of balance and coordination, they performed no better in tests of academic ability. For a child who has reading problems only, these therapies are valueless.

Motion-sickness pills

Despite the claims made by Dr. Harold Levinson in his books and during his television appearances, there is no scientific evidence to show that administering motion-sickness pills will help children with reading. In fact, these pills tend to make children sleepy, which certainly won't help their performance at school.

Patterning

Patterning is the therapy advocated by Glenn Doman and Carl Delacato. This therapy has been promoted as a treatment for everything from mental retardation to learning disorders to food allergies. It is an intensive treatment that requires parents, sometimes with a team of helpers, to repeat certain activities with their children up to four times a day. The child must go through activities such as rolling, crawling, standing, and walking in sequence over and over again. The idea is to repeat the normal pattern of human development that the child should have gone through in infancy. Repeating this "pattern" is supposed to imprint the developmental stages on to the central nervous system and correct problems related to the brain. Sensory-stimulation exercises and breathing exercises may also be part of the therapy.

The effectiveness of patterning is not supported by any scientific research and has been discredited in several clinical trials. As long ago as 1982, the American Association of Pediatrics stated firmly that not only were the claims about patterning unproven, but also that "the demands on families are so great that in some cases there may be harm in its use." Nevertheless, the therapy is still offered by the Institute for Human Potential and elsewhere, and has even been promoted on television programs.

Chiropractic

You may see advertisements circulated by chiropractors offering treatments for dyslexia and other learning disabilities. These treatments go by a number of different names. In the 1980s, chiropractor Carl Ferreri wrote a book advocating a treatment he called "applied kinesiology." His ideas have since been published on the World Wide Web, but today they usually go by the name "neural organization technique" (NOT). The therapy involves manipulating and supposedly "realigning" the bones of the head. There are no randomized controlled trials that show these techniques to be of any value to children with dyslexia. Indeed, since the bones in the head do not move, there is very little point manipulating them. Attempting to do so may be very painful for the child involved, and potentially harmful. Dr. Ferreri was once sued by several families for causing unnecessary physical pain to the children he tried to treat using this method.

What is the long-term outlook for a child with dyslexia?

Reading problems do not "disappear," nor can they be "cured." A dyslexic child will grow up to be a dyslexic adult. However, with proper reading remediation over the course of several years, dyslexic children can keep up in school and, if they wish, go on to university and postgraduate studies. I have met many people who were diagnosed as dyslexic and have learned to cope with the problem, sometimes moving into careers that involved large amounts of reading. They may read more slowly than others, and reading may never be quite as automatic for them as it is for non-dyslexic people, but it is no longer a barrier in life.

Followup studies have tested dyslexic adults who were taught as children to read using phonics. In one study, 30 percent of the adults were reading as well as an average non-dyslexic adult. In another study, 20 percent were actually reading better than average. Those who stayed in school the longest did best. Studies have also found that teenagers and adults can continue to improve their reading-comprehension and word-recognition skills. Learning to read is not a process that ends at the end of elementary school.

On the other hand, adults who did not stay in school and who never mastered reading skills continue to have problems. They struggle to read signs, menus, contracts, and instructions. They do not read magazines, newspapers, or books for pleasure. They may have dropped out of school, which reduces their chances of finding a good job. Many take up manual work. The unemployment rate for adults with reading problems is higher than that for other adults: in one study conducted in 1995, the unemployment rate for dyslexic adults was 15 percent, compared with 9 percent for non-dyslexic adults.

What happened to John, the dyslexic boy I interviewed? I talked to his teacher. She understood the problem, but said she simply did not have the time or experience to deal with John herself. She suggested I talk to the school principal. The principal agreed to have a special-education teacher spend some time with John and the teacher to get a phonics program started. John's parents also agreed to help out at home.

For the next six months, John worked on learning how to sound out words. He stayed in his regular class. His parents chose books that they knew would interest him—books on sports and exciting adventure stories. They read together several times a week. At the end of the year, John passed Grade 5. When I saw him after six months, his reading had improved by a full grade. The teacher also told me that he was much better behaved in classes where the children had to do silent reading. His math had also improved, because the teacher gave him a little longer to read the problems and had told him that if he was still having difficulty, he could ask another child to read the problem to him. John felt much happier and more confident. He was starting to enjoy going to school again.

Despite this progress, I encouraged John's parents to continue their reading remediation sessions so that he could catch up completely and keep up with his peers. The school had decided that John was no longer in need of special education, because there were other children with severe reading problems who were more in need of the extra help. By this time, however, the parents were getting quite skilled at the phonics approach and were glad to continue. After another six months, I met John again. He was now reading almost at the grade level of the rest of his class.

3

Problems with Writing, Spelling, and Math

Writing problems: dysgraphia

When I was training to become a pediatrician, I became very curious about a fellow pediatrician-in-training called Stephen who never wrote anything on paper. He used a portable type-writer for everything—patient reports, even short notes. After a while, my curiosity got the better of me, and I asked him why he typed all his written work instead of writing or printing.

His answer surprised me. He replied that he simply *couldn't* write or print clearly. No matter how hard he tried, he could-n't write anything in a way that anyone else could under-stand. Even he couldn't read his own handwriting. He had no difficulties reading, but writing in longhand was out of the question.

The problem had surfaced in elementary school. He had been doing well and getting high marks in the early grades, but in Grade 4 or 5, when he had to do more written assignments, his marks plummeted. Finally, his Grade 5 teacher called his parents and asked them to come in for a meeting at the school.

She explained that Stephen was failing at school because he could not get his ideas down on paper in such a way that anyone else could read them. Yet he was bright and capable of excellent work. She asked Stephen's parents to buy him a portable typewriter and said that she would teach him to type. His parents agreed.

Thanks to a thoughtful, caring teacher, Stephen typed his way through school, university, medical school, and on into professional life. He's probably using a laptop computer and a dictaphone now and I'm sure he has one of those electronic appointment books. Getting through life without writing is easier now than it used to be.

Stephen is one of the reasons I became interested in learning problems. I was struck by the way in which he had overcome a problem that might have defeated other people, and by the good sense of his teacher, who recognized the problem and took practical steps to deal with it. She didn't spend fruitless hours trying to improve his penmanship, she simply bypassed the problem and opened up the way for success.

Why some children can't write

Think of all the elements that come together when you sit down to write something as simple as a check or a shopping list. You need reasonably clear vision, fine motor skills, a knowledge of language and spelling, and a brain able to coordinate your ideas with your eyes and your hands to produce writing. Problems with any of these elements can make writing difficult or impossible.

For example, children with severe neurological problems will have difficulty writing, as with so many things. Cerebral palsy that affects the arms or any neurological problems that affect eye–hand coordination can reduce the ability to write. However, these problems affect many aspects of learning and development, not just writing.

A specific problem with writing, or *dysgraphia*, is not rare, although it is not as common as dyslexia. Certain children who have no other learning disabilities may have problems writing, just as Stephen did. They are not dyslexic, they have no other problems with coordination or fine motor skills, but they cannot master the skill of handwriting.

Because the problem is less common, it has not been studied as extensively as dyslexia. However, it seems likely that the cause is a subtle alteration in the brain, which is probably genetic, like dyslexia. More research is needed in this area to pinpoint the exact nature of the difference in the brains of people with dysgraphia.

The difference between bad handwriting and dysgraphia

Let's face it: handwriting is not a particularly valued skill these days. In a world of telephones, voice mail, e-mail, word processing, electronic daytimers, Palm Pilots, automatic teller machines, and other technology, most people can get through the day without ever putting pen to paper, except perhaps to sign a credit-card receipt.

Even before technology made handwriting unnecessary, schools had largely abandoned the teaching of penmanship. Gone are the days when first graders with chubby pencils spent hours practicing circles and loops on specially ruled paper, carefully keeping between the lines. The Palmer, Peterson, Stillman, and other methods for teaching cursive writing have disappeared, along with the arcane methods for forming letters such as capitals F, G, or I. The philosophy that prevails is that what children write is more important than how they write it. As a result, many children have little or no instruction in writing and simply continue to print in single, detached letters until junior high, at which point they start to produce assignments on a word processor.

Given the modern increase in poor handwriting, the problem of dysgraphia may not seem all that important. However, because children are expected to take notes in class and complete assignments by hand, and because most tests and examinations have to be written, dysgraphia may be a serious barrier to succeeding at school. Children with dysgraphia cannot create readable letters except with great difficulty. It takes them forever to get things on paper. When they try to write quickly, they produce only an illegible scrawl. For a bright child who can read well and is capable of producing good work, dysgraphia can be painfully frustrating.

Making the diagnosis of dysgraphia

Doctors and educators disagree about what is needed to make a diagnosis of dysgraphia. Some recommend a battery of psychological tests, assessments by occupational therapists, and visits to specialists or chiropractors.

I am among those who do not share this view. Just as Stephen was correctly diagnosed by an observant teacher, I believe that dysgraphia can be identified by a doctor or educator based on an assessment of the child's overall growth and development, and the records of the child's school performance.

Let me give you an example. I was asked to see Richard, a boy in Grade 6, who was having great difficulty in school. He had been promoted over the last few years, but it was clear that unless something were done, he would fail Grade 6. After I had reviewed Richard's report cards and the results of tests that Richard had taken at school, I made an appointment to talk to Richard and his parents.

I began by asking Richard about his problems at school. He said that he just thought he was "dumb." He said that he had been trying to improve for a long time, but now things were so hard that he was just about ready to give up. He said that his teacher told him that he was lazy and that many of the other kids in his class were teasing him.

At this point his parents said that Richard was certainly intelligent. It bothered them that he thought of himself as stupid. Nevertheless, they could not understand why he seemed to be unable to complete his assignments and why he was failing his written tests. They had begun to wonder about attention deficit hyperactivity disorder (ADHD). They even wondered if the teacher was right and Richard was just plain lazy.

I asked Richard to describe a typical school day for him, subject by subject. It was clear that he was indeed very bright. He was probably one grade level ahead of the rest of his class in math and he said that he loved to read and was a good reader. He pointed out that he also did well in art, in music, in phys. ed., and in drama.

I asked the parents about Richard's reading. They said that when Richard picked up a novel that he enjoyed reading, he could sit there for hours without moving. This made the diagnosis of ADHD most unlikely.

It was becoming obvious that Richard's problem was with writing. I asked him if he had trouble copying material that the teacher wrote on the blackboard. He said yes. In fact, in the time it took the other children to write down everything that the teacher had put on the board, Richard could copy down only about half the material. He also had trouble reading over his own notes. When he had to study that material for homework the same night if he was tested on that material the next day, his marks would be low because his notes were incomplete and illegible.

In addition, he did poorly when he had to write essay questions on a test. Richard had so much trouble putting things down on paper that he could get down only about half the material that he knew in a manner that could be read by anyone else. This happened even when he knew the information well and had a lot to say in answer to the questions.

At this point I told Richard and his parents that he had dysgraphia, a problem putting written material down on paper. I pointed out that many very intelligent people had the same problem, and that there were excellent ways of overcoming this problem.

I cannot see what would have been gained by requiring Richard to undergo psychological tests or assessments by specialists. Nobody doubted his intelligence, and all the evidence showed that his problems were related to his inability to write clearly. The clear priority was to start remedying the problem immediately, before Richard fell farther behind or got so frustrated at school that he gave up trying to succeed.

These are the basic steps I go through when interviewing a child who is having difficulty in school:

1. I ask the child to describe a typical school day, so I can find out which subjects are difficult. A child with dysgraphia will usually have problems in classes such as English, social studies, and science, where writing is required. As the child talks, I am also able to get a sense of the child's ability to articulate his or her thoughts.
2. I ask the child about reading and look at the report cards to see if reading is a problem, to eliminate the possibility that the problem is dyslexia, or even a general developmental problem that would make all aspects of schoolwork difficult.

3. I ask the parents about the child's ability to concentrate on tasks that he or she enjoys, such as reading, board games, artwork, or other things that require sustained effort, to rule out the likelihood of ADHD.

4. I ask the child what happens when he or she has to copy down material from the blackboard. Children with dysgraphia write very slowly, and most say that they cannot keep up with the rest of the class. Also, they may not be able to read over what they have written, especially if they try to write faster.

5. I ask about tests and exams. Children with dysgraphia often fail to complete essay questions, even if they know the material well. It takes them too long to write down what they know.

Once it is clear that the problem is with writing, I suggest that the parents and child take immediate steps to deal with the difficulty.

How teachers and parents can help a child with dysgraphia

There are no randomized controlled trials of writing remediation, as there are for reading remediation. Most experts feel that the best approach to dysgraphia is simply to bypass the problem, that is, to use technology to allow the child to do schoolwork without struggling to write in longhand.

There are two parts to this approach. Children write for two reasons: to capture information they need to learn (taking notes) and to demonstrate their knowledge of a subject (writing tests).

Instead of writing notes by hand, children can

- ask the teacher for a photocopy of the teacher's notes or ask to photocopy the notes of another child who has good handwriting; they can rely on these and on textbooks for studying;

- learn to type and use a portable typewriter or laptop computer for making notes at home and completing assignments;
- use a tape recorder to capture information in lectures.

Instead of writing tests in longhand, they can

- take tests orally;
- take multiple-choice tests;
- type out take-home or in-class tests.

If these strategies are not possible for some reason, children with dysgraphia should be allowed extra time for writing tests and exams.

The benefit of this approach is that it makes an immediate difference to the child. Rather than struggling to master a skill they find extremely difficult, and which they may rarely need to use when they move into adulthood, they can concentrate on learning other skills and can start to demonstrate what they know. This makes them feel better about school and about themselves. There is no reason to deny a bright child the opportunity to be successful in school. Moreover, because education is so important to a child's future, it is not worth the risk of letting the child become increasingly frustrated and turned off by schoolwork.

I suggested to Richard's parents that they ask his teacher to give him photocopied notes and give him oral or multiple-choice tests instead of written tests. I suggested that his parents teach Richard how to type and that he be allowed to type his home assignments. I also suggested that, if in-class, written tests are necessary, Richard be given extra time to complete the written material.

I was pleased that Richard's principal and teachers accepted these recommendations. His parents made sure he was taught to type and that he had a word processor to use at home. Richard's performance at school improved considerably. His teachers realized that he was actually a gifted student and provided him with considerable support. His anxiety and depression disappeared and he passed Grade 6 with excellent marks.

Spelling problems: dysorthographia

Most children with dyslexia have difficulty learning to spell. The best approach for these children is to concentrate on improving their reading ability using reading remediation and phonics. As their reading improves, so will their spelling.

Occasionally, however, I have seen children whose problem is with spelling only. They have no difficulty reading, but on spelling tests and in written assignments they lose marks because they cannot seem to remember the correct spelling of words. The cause of this particular problem, which is officially known as "dysorthographia," is unknown, although it does appear to run in families, like dyslexia.

Admittedly, spelling in English is not easy to learn. As soon as a child masters a particular spelling rule, he or she will immediately encounter a host of exceptions to the rule. Phonetics is no guide to spelling in a language full of silent letters (*comb, knife*), homonyms (*hoard, horde*), inconsistencies relating to double letters (*excel, cell*), and numerous ways of spelling the same sound (*siege, seize, cede, seed, seat,* and so on). Even adults wrestle with correct spelling of certain words. I often have to stop and check the correct spelling of many medical terms.

English spelling is so inconsistent that there are at least half a dozen organizations, such as the Simplified Spelling Society and the Uniform English Society, trying to promote standardized spelling. The idea is not new. Benjamin Franklin, Mark

Twain, George Bernard Shaw, and Noah Webster (of Webster's Dictionary) are among those who have advocated simplifying the spelling of English. The idea is to make it more like languages such as Spanish, where most words are spelled just as they are pronounced. A few simplified spellings, such as *thru*, *nite*, and *catalog*, get used occasionally, but the movement hasn't made much headway. Part of the problem may be that the various organizations cannot agree on just which phonetic spellings they would use.

Difficult as English may be, most children eventually develop a sense for how most words look when they are spelled correctly. However, some children never develop this knack. This disability is much less serious than dyslexia. It looms large at school, where emphasis is placed on correct spelling, but, in later life, it poses fewer problems. You probably have friends and colleagues who confess that they are terrible spellers, but who nevertheless have successful careers. Quite a few professional writers are poor spellers. They rely on computer spell checkers and professional editors to correct their work for them.

Perhaps the one place where spelling is important today is on the World Wide Web. Finding information often relies on the ability to key in a series of letters correctly, either as the name of a Web site, or in a search string. If you need information on, say, Kazakhstan, you need to be able to type it correctly.

Helping a child with spelling problems

I was once asked to see a girl called Bridget, who was in Grade 6. She read well, had good marks in math, and she had no trouble getting her ideas down on paper. However, whenever she had to complete her written work in class, she lost marks for poor spelling. She did better on written homework assignments, because at home she checked everything carefully with a dictionary. The problem was making her anxious at school. She dreaded tests and exams, and was in despair about how to improve her marks. She was bright and good at schoolwork, but her marks suffered because of her problems with spelling.

There are two ways to approach a problem like Bridget's. The first approach would be to give her intensive instruction in memory training to improve her spelling. This approach can be successful, under certain circumstances. In a study conducted in 1988, researchers in Maryland and Montana worked with children who were poor spellers. The children were divided into two groups randomly. One group worked on memory-training strategies. The strategy required them to say the word, write it down while saying it aloud, check the spelling, trace it and say it over again, and finally write it from memory and recheck the spelling. The second group was an attention placebo group. They were given spelling games, but no extra help in learning to spell.

The group that received instruction in memory training improved their spelling, provided that the teacher made sure that they learned each word using the special strategy. If they stopped using the strategy, their spelling did not improve relative to the children in the control group. Unfortunately, the study did not follow up these children, so we do not know if the improvements lasted after the teacher stopped monitoring those who were using the memory-training strategy. Nor did the study find out whether the children were able to apply the techniques to new words, beyond those used in the study, and without the teacher's supervision.

It is quite possible that poor spellers can improve their spelling using a strategy like the one in the study, but it requires a lot of time on the part of the teacher. If there are only a few poor spellers in a large class, most teachers would not consider this the best use of their time. The strategy might be better for parents to try with their children after school.

The second way to approach a spelling problem is to bypass it. This is what I suggested to Bridget's parents and teacher. I asked the teacher to allow Bridget to use a small spelling dictionary in class and to take it into tests and exams, so that she could check her spelling. I also recommended that Bridget's parents teach her to type and let her do her homework assignments on their home computer, using a word-processing program with a spell-check feature.

Bridget's parents and teachers accepted my suggestions, and Bridget's marks began to improve immediately. She felt better about her schoolwork and about herself.

Using the right tools

As we all know, using an ordinary dictionary requires enough knowledge of spelling to know where to look up a word. However, special spelling dictionaries allow children to look up a phonetic approximation of the word to find the correct spelling. These dictionaries would, for example, list a phonetic spelling such as "nok" and show its correct spelling as "knock."

Most computer spell checkers are not quite as accommodating. The average spell checker cannot correct a word if the misspelling creates a different word (such as typing "red" when the correct word should be "read") and it cannot provide any guidance if the word keyed in is too far from its correct spelling. There are, however, software programs and small computers the size of calculators that can match a phonetic spelling with its correct spelling. Type in "nok," press the Spell key, and the computer will produce "knock."

Spelling dictionaries and computerized spell checkers can be very useful for poor spellers and allow them to concentrate on what they are trying to say in their written work. Bypassing the problem can bring about an immediate improvement in children's schoolwork and in their self-esteem.

Problems with mathematics: dyscalculia

Even though there are gaps in our understanding of problems with reading and writing, there is increasing research on these learning disorders. Problems with mathematics, however, have not been studied as intensively, and much less is known about their causes and effects.

It is a little surprising that so little has been done, since using numbers is almost as important an everyday skill as reading. We all need to manage our money, from paying the rent to paying taxes, from calculating a restaurant tip to comparison shopping. We all have to keep track of dozens of numbers, from telephone numbers to personal identification numbers for the bank machine. Most jobs require some ability to handle numbers, and the self-employed have to understand the financial side of their businesses.

Perhaps one reason for the lack of understanding of math problems is the complex nature of mathematics itself. Think about all the elements involved in becoming proficient in this subject at elementary school. Mathematics involves

- reading, writing, and other language skills;
- an ability to distinguish relative sizes and quantities of objects;
- an ability to identify sequences, patterns, and groups;
- an ability to use abstract symbols to represent objects;
- arithmetic skills, or the ability to add, subtract, multiply, and divide;

- reasoning skills, or the ability to know when and how to use these operations in solving a mathematical problem;
- spatial understanding, needed in geometry and in understanding concepts such as area and volume;
- an understanding of proportions and ratios;
- long-term memory for formulas, times tables, and elements of mathematics that are used repeatedly;
- short-term memory to hold the elements of a math problem in mind while working on its solution;
- an ability to understand purely abstract ideas, such as negative numbers or number systems that do not use base ten.

And that's just for starters. These skills will see a child through to about Grade 4. By Grade 5, children are required to carry out complicated operations involving fractions and decimals, percentages, metric conversions, averages, equations, and a wide variety of geometrical shapes. Quite a few parents I've talked to are intimidated by the Grade 5 math curriculum, and sometimes are unable to help their children when they have difficulty completing a math homework assignment.

Clearly, to talk about "mathematical problems" is to lump together a host of possible problems. For example, one student may cope well with geometry, but may be floored by algebra. Another may be good with practical problems involving money or visible objects, but may be stumped by purely abstract mathematical operations. Many people have differing abilities in the many elements that make up the complex subject known as mathematics.

This complexity has probably hampered researchers who have tried to determine the number of children suffering from a specific learning disability in mathematics. One study by Varda Gross-Tsur and colleagues found that 6 percent of Grade 5 children were scoring at least two grade levels below

Grade 5 in mathematics. However, within this group 17 percent had reading problems, and 26 percent suffered from attention deficit hyperactivity disorder (ADHD), so the number of children who are having problems with mathematics alone must be less than 6 percent. In another study by Linda Siegel and myself, children who had average reading ability but were having difficulty with math were found to have problems putting things down on paper. Finally, a study by C. Lewis and colleagues found that about 1.3 percent of children have a problem with mathematics that cannot be traced to a reading or attentional problem and 2.3 percent had a problem with mathematics and reading. The study did not look at the children's writing skills.

Dyscalculia: a specific math difficulty

Although many problems can interfere with the ability to understand and succeed in mathematics, the term "dyscalculia" usually refers to a particular problem calculating, or performing the arithmetic operations of addition, subtraction, multiplication, and division. This problem may exist independently of the ability to understand mathematical concepts or to handle the abstractions required in mathematics.

Just as the teaching of reading has changed over the past few decades, the teaching of mathematics has changed. Around the time that phonics was losing ground to whole language, arithmetic drills were giving way to teaching methods that emphasized problem solving and the underlying concepts of mathematics. Most children now spend less time practicing what used to be called "mental arithmetic" and memorizing the times tables. Given the lack of research in this area, it is difficult to say whether this change has made life harder for children with dyscalculia.

Making the diagnosis of dyscalculia

Jessica is a ten-year-old girl in Grade 5. Her parents brought her to see me because she seemed unable to make any progress in her math class. Her teacher kept her after school to go over problems with her, and her parents spent hours helping her with her mathematics homework, but she was still struggling to keep up with the rest of her class.

When I read through Jessica's reports and interviewed Jessica and her parents, I could tell that she was an intelligent girl. Her reading and writing skills were average for her age, and she did not have any problems with attention or concentration in class or at home.

I asked Jessica to describe a typical school day for me. She said that she was doing reasonably well in most subjects, but she felt really stupid in her math class. I asked her to do some reading for me and she was clearly at least at her grade level, if not ahead. In addition, her reading comprehension was excellent.

Then I gave her a paper and pencil and asked her to solve the following problem: "Farmer Jones has 25 acres of land and each acre produces 20 bushels of corn. How many bushels of corn could Farmer Jones produce each year?" She tried very hard to find the answer but could not. When I asked her what she would have to do to solve the problem, she said she understood that she would have to multiply 25 by 20, but she couldn't do the calculation. I gave her my hand calculator and she got the answer immediately.

I gave her another problem to solve. Once again, she could not solve it with a pencil and paper, although she knew the operation she had to perform to get the answer. As soon as she was allowed to use the calculator, she solved the problem. After a few more problems, it was clear where the problem lay.

I told Jessica and her parents that Jessica had a problem with calculating. I added that it had nothing to do with Jessica's intelligence and that some very intelligent people have trouble doing math. Nor did it mean that Jessica was lazy. She was working very hard, but her disability, which was probably inherited, was holding her back.

Helping a child with dyscalculia

As with writing and spelling problems, there are two possible approaches: one can either offer some form of intensive math remediation, or bypass the problem.

There are only a few studies on math remediation. One looked at a technique called "team-assisted individualization." This approach uses peer tutoring to help children who are having difficulty. Peer tutoring is based on the idea that different students learn at different rates. At any given time, some students will have mastered a new skill or a new area of knowledge while others are still struggling with it.

In a study conducted by Slavin, Madden, and Leavey in 1984, students in several Grade 3, 4, and 5 math classes were divided into small groups. Within each group, the students helped each other and the teacher moved from group to group, overseeing their work and helping out when the students in the group were having difficulties. The study also built in an incentive to encourage the students to work together. The teacher rewarded students only when *all* the students in the group performed well. That way, the students who did well in math had a good reason to help the weaker students.

By the end of the study, all the children in the class had improved in math, both those with learning problems in math and those who had no learning problems. The study had some flaws: children were not randomly selected for participation, and there was no attention placebo group with which to compare the students. Nevertheless, the approach did seem to help all students improve their performance in math.

This approach might work well in schools, but it does require special training for the teacher. Moreover, the teachers in the study were motivated by the regular visits of the researchers to their classrooms.

A few studies have also been done on the use of computer programs that help teach math skills. The results are inconclusive, but if the child benefits from routine practice and math drills, he or she may prefer to do these drills on a computer rather than with pencil and paper. Computer programs can give immediate feedback on a child's performance and may incorporate colorful visual elements that make them more enjoyable to use. If a child who is having difficulty with math has access to a computer, computer-assisted math remediation should certainly be tried.

However, if the child simply has a problem with calculating and not with mathematical concepts as a whole, the best approach may simply be to bypass the problem. In other words, give her a small calculator and teach her how to use it. This is what I suggested to Jessica and her parents. I also discussed this with Jessica's teacher, who agreed. Jessica's progress in math began to improve at once and she started to feel better about herself and about school.

I generally recommend bypassing this type of problem because I do not see a lot of value in subjecting a child to intensive remediation when a simple, inexpensive calculator is very effective in dealing with everyday math. Students in high school and university routinely use calculators in their mathematics and science classes. Most adults, including those who work in fields such as accounting or engineering, go through life never doing calculations in their head or with pencil and paper. We all use calculators, spreadsheets, and software to do calculations for us.

The most important part of studying mathematics is to understand the principles and concepts. Jessica knew when she had to use multiplication and when it was necessary to divide one number by another. She knew how numbers related to each other; all she couldn't do was the actual calculation to get the answer. Once she was able to use a calculator, she was able to demonstrate her mastery of the concepts and principles of mathematics.

Children with other kinds of math problems

Much more research needs to be done to understand the problems of children who have difficulty with math. Children may have specific disabilities relating to the use of abstract symbols, or to spatial reasoning, or to understanding mathematical concepts. These difficulties are not well understood, and there is very little research on the best way to help children with these problems.

If your child or a student in your class has a math problem, you may need to carry out a little research on your own. Where does the child run into difficulty? Is the problem with written work only, or both oral and written work? Does the child understand a mathematical problem that involves real objects, but finds purely abstract calculations difficult? Can he remember numbers accurately? Does she have trouble interpreting diagrams or solving problems that involve spatial relations? Is the problem with the method of teaching? Would a different approach help the child understand?

At the same time, find out what the child *can* do. Can she draw pictures to help herself solve problems? Has she developed coping strategies for remembering numbers or concepts?

Is he able to understand numbers in contexts outside math class (baseball statistics, data on car engines)? Helping children with any kind of learning disability means making a bridge between what they have already mastered and what they find difficult.

The most important thing to remember is to intervene before the child becomes so frustrated that he or she gives up in despair and accepts failure. Helping a child to overcome a problem will boost the child's confidence in all areas.

4

Attention Deficit Hyperactivity Disorder

Look into an ordinary Grade 3 classroom. The teacher is at the front, giving a lesson on fractions. Most of the children are sitting at their desks, facing the teacher. But one child is staring out the window. Another is on the floor, perhaps searching for a dropped pencil. A third is furiously scribbling on some paper. Two kids at the back are whispering to each other. Suddenly a child interrupts the teacher, asking to leave the room.

Now look into a conference room at a typical business event. A speaker stands at the lectern beside an overhead projector, describing a new approach to human-resources management. Most of the business people present are looking at the speaker, and some are making notes. However, one has fallen asleep, head nodding, in the second row. Another is tapping away on a laptop, perhaps preparing a presentation for later in the day. A third is drawing elaborate doodles on a pad of paper. At the back, someone talks into a cellphone.

Suddenly a man in the third row stands up abruptly, knocking over a coffee cup, and walks out of the room.

Two very ordinary scenes, in which children and adults are required to sit still and listen. Invariably, some of them can't seem to do this. Why?

It may be that some of the children and some of the business people have attention deficit hyperactivity disorder (ADHD), which makes it hard for them to sit still and concentrate. It is equally possible that none of them has a clinical disorder, and that those who are not paying attention are simply bored, overtired, restless, preoccupied, or in urgent need of a bathroom break.

There are two schools of thought about ADHD. One says that ADHD is overdiagnosed and that ADHD medications are overprescribed, and that really only a small percentage of people actually has the disorder. Some people who agree with this analysis point to the influence of the television, videos, and computer games, which are designed to jump from image to image and soundbite to soundbite, and which tend to fragment the attention and overstimulate the mind. They suggest that these influences make normal children behave in a way that seems hyperactive, which may swell the numbers of those demonstrating the symptoms associated with ADHD.

The other group says that ADHD is underdiagnosed and that it is a more common disorder than is generally thought. Television and computer games may produce similar behavior in some people, but ADHD is still a genuine, clinical problem, and many people could benefit from appropriate ADHD treatment.

One reason for the controversy over ADHD is that definitions of the disorder vary. Surveys of teachers that require them to rate the behavior of the children in their classrooms and identify the proportion with ADHD get varying results, because different researchers use a different cutoff point to distinguish "normally" active, impulsive, distractible children, from "abnormal" levels of hyperactivity, impulsiveness, or inattentiveness.

Moreover, ADHD may take different forms in different children. A few years ago, the condition was known as ADD, or attention deficit disorder, but researchers now include "hyperactivity" in the name. This may obscure the fact that some children are inattentive and impulsive but not hyperactive. These children have a disorder that interferes with learning in school, but their problems are not as obvious as those of hyperactive children.

The question remains: is ADHD a medical fad or an epidemic? It is neither. It is a distinct, identifiable medical disorder that tends to run in families. Although much of the public awareness of the problem has focused on North America and the fact that more than 1.5 million children in the United States alone are receiving medication for the disorder, ADHD is not a North American problem. It is found in children all around the world.

If you suspect that your child or one of your students may have ADHD, your first step is to learn more about the disorder before jumping to conclusions. The next step is to have the child evaluated by a physician. Don't be too quick to slap a label on any child, but, at the same time, don't ignore behavior that may signal a problem that could interfere with the child's schooling and later success in life.

Defining the problem

Just what is ADHD, anyway? In general, there are three kinds of behavior associated with the disorder:

- inattentiveness or distractibility;

- impulsiveness;
- hyperactivity.

These problems may occur singly or in combination. However, any one of them will interfere with learning.

ADHD has something in common with dyslexia in that paying attention, concentrating, and controlling impulses are forms of learned behavior. Children do not do these things naturally; they must learn to do them as they grow up, just as they learn to read and write. ADHD interferes with the process of acquiring these skills, just as dyslexia interferes with the process of learning to read and write.

Let's take a closer look at each of the behaviors associated with ADHD.

Inattentiveness or distractibility

We all daydream. We all find our minds wandering at times. We all get distracted by minor annoyances. We all procrastinate now and then. We all have times when we can't seem to focus on a task when there are other things to do that are more interesting, or when the way ahead is not clear. However, most of us learn to put aside daydreams while there is work to be done, to get on with the task at hand and concentrate for as long as necessary to get it finished, so we can move on to something we enjoy more.

However, for the ADHD child or adult, putting aside daydreams, blocking out distractions, and focusing on routine tasks seem to be impossible. Some children with the disorder daydream constantly, unaware of their surroundings. Their minds wander off in class, or when someone is talking to them. They do not hear what is said to them. They may even start talking about what is in their minds, which may have nothing to do with what is going on around them. When this behavior is consistent and uncontrolled, it may indicate ADHD.

Another symptom is the inability to screen out minor distractions. A child in class may be distracted by traffic outside the window, by the sounds of other children turning pages or shifting in their seats, by voices out in the hallway, or simply by the colors and shapes of the posters on the walls. Children who are extremely easily distracted can be overwhelmed in places full of noise and movement, such as a busy shopping street or mall, or at a boisterous birthday party.

Children with ADHD may also drift from one activity to another as they encounter distractions. For example, a family is just about to leave to go on a picnic. The mother asks her little boy to fetch his hat from his room. He wanders off. Ten minutes later, the family is still waiting and the boy's sister goes in search of him. She finds him playing with the cat. He had entered his room, seen the cat, and forgotten the errand.

Inattention often means that children with ADHD are forever losing possessions or forgetting what they have been told to do. They forget to bring home what they need to do their homework, or they lose toys and clothing. Because they have trouble listening, they have difficulty following instructions. They seem perpetually disorganized.

There are a few situations in which a child with ADHD may appear to be concentrating, but really is not. One is watching television. Although the child may sit through a half-hour television program, he or she is simply being distracted by the constantly changing images on the screen. Another is playing computer and video games. Again, the images change rapidly and the need to press keys or manipulate a joystick keeps the child busy. In these situations, the children are responding to the stimulation of distracting images and movement. However, when it comes to quiet activities that require real concentration, such as reading or drawing, the child usually can't seem to sit still.

Impulsiveness

We often tell children "Look before you leap." However, ADHD children seem to have difficulty following this advice. They rush headlong through life, seemingly unable to plan ahead or foresee the consequences of their actions. When an idea comes into their head, or they decide they want something, they act immediately and single-mindedly. They want something and they want it *now*. If thwarted, they may cry or throw a tantrum. No matter how often you tell them to wait their turn, think before they act, or listen to directions before charging ahead, they keep rushing into things.

It doesn't help that the media and consumer society in general seem to encourage instant gratification. Advertisers spend millions of dollars on research into ways to make children want to possess the things they see on television. The psychological manipulation of children by advertisers and the media is designed to turn even non-ADHD children into single-minded consumers. It's a part of modern life that I find quite disturbing. A friend of mine who used to work in a toy store once told me that many children seemed to leave the store in tears, because they were forced to choose only one toy, or because they were there to pick out a birthday present for another child and not for themselves. After weeks of watching ads on television that filled their minds with product names and promises of excitement, they were distraught because they could not have the toys that they'd seen on television. Teaching self-restraint is an uphill job for parents these days.

However, for the child with ADHD, impulsiveness is not just a matter of wanting things they see on television. These children are impulsive in all areas of life. They interrupt conversations, blurt out the answers to questions in class without putting up their hands, push others aside to get what they want, and have difficulty taking turns at games or in structured activities at school. Sometimes they say the first thing that comes into their head, even if it insults or offends the person they are speaking to. A friend of mine used to joke, "Please make sure brain is engaged before putting mouth into gear." Children with ADHD can't seem to manage this feat. They speak or act first and think later, or not at all.

Impulsive, sometimes aggressive behavior understandably annoys other children and may be the reason why some children with ADHD have difficulty making or keeping friends.

Hyperactivity

A hyperactive child is usually a fidgety child. He squirms in his chair, jumps up from the dinner table frequently, taps his fingers on his school desk, swings his legs, fiddles with pencils or pens, shuffles papers and books. He may talk constantly.

Teachers find this kind of behavior disruptive because classroom work often requires children to work quietly at their desks. They may be the first to notice and complain about the child's behavior. Parents, however, may have a greater tolerance for hyperactivity, particularly if they tend to be very active themselves. Some households I have visited are full of movement, sounds, and chatter, and a child who is constantly in motion doesn't stand out much against the background activity level. However, in a classroom, a library, or at church, synagogue, or mosque, the ADHD child who cannot sit quietly stands out.

Three forms of ADHD

The American Psychiatric Association has identified three different types of ADHD:

- ADHD that involves all three symptoms: inattentiveness, impulsiveness, and hyperactivity;
- ADHD in which the predominant characteristic is inattentiveness;
- ADHD in which the predominant characteristics are impulsiveness and hyperactivity.

In surveys of children with ADHD, it usually appears that more boys than girls suffer from the disorder. However, in recent years it has become apparent that hyperactivity may not be present. Now more girls are being diagnosed as having the second type of ADHD.

How common is ADHD?

There is no consensus on what proportion of the population suffers from the disorder. One researcher carried out a survey of teachers in the Ottawa–Carleton area, using the Conners rating scale. This is a checklist of behavior symptoms associated with hyperactivity and inattention. Altogether, more than 14,000 children were rated by their teachers. The researcher found that results from the Ottawa school board suggested that 15 percent of the children had the problem, whereas results from the Carleton school board suggested that only 12 percent were affected. Depending on what types of behavior are considered symptomatic of ADHD, the figures from different surveys conducted by different researchers in different cities and countries range from a low of 5 percent to a high of 22 percent.

What we do know is that 3 to 4 percent of children between the ages of five and fourteen in the United States are currently receiving medication for ADHD. However, even this figure may not be an accurate guide to the prevalence of the problem, because some doctors may be overprescribing medication and others underprescribing it, depending on their attitudes toward the disorder. I think it is quite likely that the real figure for children with ADHD is about 5 percent. This means that some children are not receiving medication who really need it and also that some children are being assigned the ADHD label when in fact they are merely rambunctious in certain situations.

It is also hard to tell how many children with ADHD also have a specific problem with reading, writing, or math. Surveys have suggested that about 25 percent of children with ADHD also suffer from dyslexia or some other specific learning disability, and that about 40 percent of those who are diagnosed with dyslexia or another specific learning problem also have ADHD. However, I suspect that these figures may be too high. A child who has difficulty concentrating will understandably do poorly in reading and math tests. However, if the concentration problem is controlled with medication, the reading or math problems may disappear. Conversely, children who have a specific learning problem such as dyslexia may be perceived by teachers as disruptive and hyperactive because they act up in class, but when their reading problem is corrected, their behavior also improves.

What causes ADHD?

Although our understanding of ADHD is far from complete, research has found that ADHD has to do with brain chemistry and function. Researchers have studied the way the blood flows in the brains of people with and without ADHD and the way the brains of different types of people use up glucose (a type of sugar). Although the studies use different techniques, it seems clear that brain function does differ noticeably in people with ADHD.

Most of the research has focused on the frontal lobes of the brain and on the role of neurotransmitters, the chemicals that transmit messages from one part of the brain to another. It is possible that ADHD is caused by a problem in transmitting messages around the brain. Different parts of the brain are concerned with motor control, with weighing the consequences before acting, with deciding which stimuli in the environment to pay attention to and which to ignore. Information comes in, but if it does not get distributed to the parts of the brain that control actions and filter out unwanted information, the result is unnecessary movement, impulsive actions, and constant distractibility.

These differences in brain function and chemistry appear to be inherited. ADHD runs in families. The evidence for this comes, in part, from twin studies. If one identical twin has ADHD, the chances are about 85 percent that the other one will too. For non-identical twins, or for siblings who are not twins, the likelihood that both have the disorder is about 30 percent.

Other studies have looked at adopted children to see if their behavior tends to repeat that of their birth parents, or if they are more influenced by the behavior of their adopted parents. This research is intended to assess the importance of the family environment in producing children with ADHD. The results confirm the genetic link, because children with ADHD tend to come from birth parents who have ADHD. If the adoptive parents have ADHD and the birth parents do not, the adoptive parents do not influence the behavior of their children so much that the children also exhibit the symptoms of ADHD.

At present, the location of the mutated gene or genes that cause ADHD has not been identified, and the role of neurotransmitters in ADHD is still not completely understood. However, research continues in this area, and future findings may lead to improved treatments for the disorder. Research is also continuing into the connection between ADHD and fetal development. Problems or events during pregnancy may affect the developing brain of the fetus and cause behavioral problems as the child grows up.

Are diet, food additives, or allergies to blame?

For years, many pediatricians believed that hyperactivity was caused by a diet high in sugar, food coloring, and other food additives. A few doctors still hold to this idea, even though randomized controlled trials have shown that diet does not play a role in causing ADHD. There are other reasons why too much sugar is unhealthy, but there is no evidence that it causes hyperactivity. As for food additives, their connection to ADHD is pure speculation, since there is no evidence that they affect brain functioning.

Nevertheless, some food faddists persist in stating that food additives are to blame for ADHD and recommending additive-free diets as a "cure" for ADHD. The most prominent is Dr. Benjamin Feingold, a pediatrician and allergist from California who published a book called *Why Your Child Is Hyperactive* in 1975. The book contained no research to back up his assertions that artificial food coloring, flavoring, and flavor enhancers cause hyperactivity, only anecdotes from his own practice.

Dr. Doris Rapp, a pediatrician and allergist who practices in Buffalo, New York, has proposed that hyperactivity and many other problems are caused by allergies to certain foods such as milk, chocolate, eggs, wheat, corn, peanuts, pork, and sugar. Her theories have not been confirmed by any scientific studies.

Although the link between allergies and learning disabilities has not been definitely established, if you suspect that your child has any kind of allergy, you should talk to your child's doctor and arrange for testing. If the child feels chronically unwell because of undiagnosed allergies, she is likely to do less than her best at school. However, if the physician feels that your child does not have allergies, there is no reason to alter the child's diet.

Is ADHD simply a product of the frenetic pace of modern life or the home environment?

Recently, a book by Dr. Gabor Maté called *Scattered Minds: A New Look at the Origins and Healing of Attention Deficit Disorder*, challenged the accepted view of ADHD. "I do not see it as a fixed, inherited brain disorder, but as a physiological consequence of life in a particular environment, in a particular culture," says Dr. Maté, who suffers from the disorder himself. Considering that all three of Dr. Maté's children also have been diagnosed with ADHD, this is a surprising statement. Dr. Maté's theory is that people inherit a predisposition to ADHD, but that the disorder is triggered by a stressful environment.

There is no question that the pace of life today is dizzying. Children today suffer from stresses that my generation never knew when we were young. No doubt some children become irritable, depressed, or aggressive because of these stresses. Our media-saturated culture may worsen the problem behavior of children with ADHD, while at the same time making the disorder harder to spot, because everything is moving so fast. But that is not the same as suggesting that these stresses and our high-tech, high-speed culture actually change the chemistry of the brain.

I also object to the idea that the environment can somehow "create" ADHD, because, if you accept this reasoning, it's a short step to saying that parents are to blame for their children's having ADHD. Although Dr. Maté insists that he is not attributing ADHD to bad parenting, he cites factors such as marital conflict, a hectic lifestyle, the parents' unresolved personal problems, and tense family relationships in the development of children's' ADHD. Saying that a stressful home environment is at fault in many cases is very close to blaming parents for ADHD.

I reject any suggestion that ADHD is the "fault" of the parents. I have seen too many exhausted parents, particularly mothers, worn out with trying to deal with their children's behavior, and close to depression because they have been told that the child's condition is the result of their own bad parenting skills. Friends, relatives, teachers, and even some pediatricians (who should know better) are often quick to criticize the parents of children with ADHD. "You should spend more time with him." "You should set clear limits, so she knows where she stands." "You shouldn't let him watch so much television." "She's just spoiled; you shouldn't indulge her so much." "It's that daycare you sent him to." "She's picking up on your tension when you come home from work." If you are the parent of a child with ADHD, no doubt you've heard all of these and more. Older, childless relatives are a particular source of useless advice.

Dr. Maté's approach echoes all the well-meaning but unhelpful comments of relatives. As far as I can see, it will make the parents of children with ADHD feel worse, not better. Not only must parents who are having marriage problems or other personal difficulties struggle to overcome them, but they are now being made to feel that their inability to solve these problems earlier or more effectively has created a serious disorder in their children. Suggesting that the parents' failure to create a stress-free, nurturing environment can trigger ADHD simply puts additional pressure on them and sets up an unrealistic goal of perfect family harmony.

Nobody could possibly object to Dr. Maté's recommendations to parents to strengthen the security of their child's relationship with them and to put the child's well-being and self-esteem ahead of behavioral goals. This is sound advice for all parents, whether or not their children have ADHD. However, placing the burden of "healing" on the parents of children with ADHD is an additional source of stress for families that are already struggling. Yes, parents can do a great deal to help their children, but they did not create the child's problems in the first place. The best available research shows clearly that ADHD is a genetic disorder, related to brain functioning, and this is what you should tell the next person who tries to suggest that it is the parents' fault.

Making the diagnosis of ADHD

Sam is a charming, bright eight-year-old who is in danger of failing Grade 3. Although he is intelligent, he can't sit still, can't wait his turn, and can't concentrate on his work. He is easily distracted and is the first one in class to stop work when there is a knock on the classroom door or someone drops a book.

Sam has no close friends, because the other children are tired of his constant interruptions and the way he sometimes interferes when other children are playing games. The teacher is annoyed because he makes careless mistakes in his written work and often fails to finish the work assigned to him. His parents are in despair about his forgetfulness and his tendency to lose things. He is always on the go, running around or talking endlessly. He never seems to listen when they talk to him. They have been told that he should either fail the year or be in full-time special education.

I was asked to see Sam at this point. His parents brought me his report cards from school, told me about the teacher's comments, and described his behavior at home. His father also told me that he had been just like Sam when he was a boy. He'd dropped out of school in Grade 10 at the age of seventeen, after failing twice. He qualified as a motor mechanic and had held down a job ever since, but he couldn't sit still for long and often feels restless.

I talked to Sam about school. He squirmed in his chair, swinging his legs back and forth, and said that he hated school. The other children were mean to him. The teacher was always yelling at him to pay attention. Then his attention was caught by something outside the window and his voice trailed off.

By this point, I was fairly sure that Sam had ADHD, but I spent some time discussing Sam's behavior with his parents and talking to the boy about school. The questions I asked were based on the *Diagnostic and Statistical Manual of Mental Disorders*, published by the American Psychiatric Association. The manual is currently in its fourth edition (1994) and is commonly referred to as *DSM-IV*. Over the course of the interview, I covered the five steps in the diagnostic process for ADHD recommended by *DSM-IV*. Here is a slightly simplified description of the steps.

Step One: Identify the symptoms

There are two lists of symptoms: one for attentional problems and another for hyperactivity and impulsiveness. If the child has *six or more* of the symptoms from *either one* of the lists, and if these symptoms are *often present* (not just occasionally) and have persisted for *at least six months*, then ADHD is suspected. The symptoms of inattention are:

- fails to pay close attention to details or makes careless mistakes in schoolwork or other activities;
- has difficulty sustaining attention in tasks or play activities;
- does not seem to listen when spoken to directly;
- does not follow through on instructions and fails to finish schoolwork or chores (but not because of a failure to understand the instructions or because of deliberate naughtiness);
- has difficulty organizing tasks and activities;
- avoids, dislikes, or is reluctant to engage in tasks that require sustained mental effort such as homework;
- loses things such as toys, school assignments, pencils, books, tools, clothes;
- is easily distracted by noises, movements, or other stimuli;
- is forgetful.

The symptoms of hyperactivity and impulsiveness are:

- fidgets with hands or feet or squirms in chairs;
- leaves seat in classroom or at the dinner table or whenever remaining seated is expected;
- runs about or climbs in situations where this behavior is inappropriate;
- has difficulty playing quietly;
- is constantly "on the go" or acts as if "driven by a motor";
- talks excessively;
- blurts out answers before questions have been completed;
- has difficulty awaiting turns in games or other structured activities;
- interrupts or intrudes on others (butts into conversations or games).

Step Two: Determine when the symptoms first appeared

If the symptoms appeared before the child was seven, ADHD may be present.

Step Three: Specify where the symptoms occur

Is the child's behavior a problem only at school or is it a problem at home as well? If the child has behavior problems in two or more settings, ADHD may be present.

Step Four: Assess the severity of the symptoms

Is the child's behavior merely annoying, or is it causing real problems for the child at school or in social situations? Before making a diagnosis of ADHD, a doctor needs clear evidence that ADHD is really impairing the child's ability to function at school or at home.

Step Five: Rule out other possible diagnoses

It is important to make sure that problem behavior is not the result of some other problem or disorder, such as global development delays or psychiatric problems.

Are other tests necessary?

By the time I had covered the five steps of the *DSM-IV* with Sam and his parents, I knew that Sam had ADHD. He had symptoms of both hyperactivity and inattention, and the symptoms had appeared before he was seven. They affected his behavior both at school and at home. They were serious enough to affect his schoolwork and put him at risk of failing his year. Also, they were affecting his self-esteem, since he didn't understand why the other children didn't like him. Finally, Sam's mother told me that he had developed normally as a baby and small child, so I knew that his problems were not the result of developmental delays. There was no evidence of depression or any other psychiatric disorder.

I did not order any further tests. There are no laboratory tests that will detect the presence of ADHD. There also seemed little point is suggesting an IQ test. From what I now knew about Sam, I could see that he was bright, but it was clear that he would do badly on a test because he was so easily distractible and tended not to finish things. IQ tests are like academic tests: they require concentration and Sam just couldn't concentrate. I told the parents about my diagnosis and we began to discuss possible treatment options.

Always get an outside opinion

I have provided a simplified version of the *DSM-IV* so that you can start thinking about the child's behavior before going for an interview with a physician. Some of these questions can't be answered quickly; you need time to consider them. You may also need input from others: teachers, babysitters, relatives. However, this is not a tool for do-it-yourself diagnosis. You should never try to diagnose a child without the help of a doctor. Not only can a doctor provide a wealth of experience to put your child's behavior in context, but doctors are a little more objective. For example, if your first child is quiet and studious and your second child is more rambunctious, you may see the second child as "abnormal" in comparison with the first. However, it is possible that the second child is also normal, just more energetic and outgoing than the first child. You need an outsider's view.

I say that doctors are "a little more objective," rather than completely objective, because the whole process depends on fairly subjective assessments. If you look at the lists of symptoms, you will see that most of them are open to interpretation. What does "talks excessively" really mean? Where does chattiness end and excessive talking begin? Or "difficulty organizing tasks"? Or "forgetfulness"? Lots of children are disorganized and forgetful—just like many adults.

The reason why no one can say for sure what proportion of children have ADHD is because different researchers draw the line in different places. Different doctors do too. Don't be afraid to get a second opinion if you think that a doctor is making too much or too little of certain behaviors.

A *different diagnosis*

In some cases, I see children who have some symptoms of ADHD, but who do not have the disorder. In these cases, I use the *DSM-IV* criteria to *rule out* the possibility of ADHD. Here's an example.

I was recently asked to see a seven-and-a-half year-old boy because his teacher was concerned that he might have hyperactivity. The child's family physician had done an initial assessment and felt that there were some characteristics of ADHD, but she wanted another opinion and referred him and his family to me.

When I looked at Neil's report card, I saw no indication from the teacher's comments that Neil was hyperactive or impulsive. However, I noticed a number of comments that suggested that his attention span was very short. I asked Neil's mother about them. She told me that Neil had had no problems concentrating on activities in kindergarten or in Grade 1. But, starting in Grade 2, the teacher had told her repeatedly that Neil often failed to pay close attention to details and made careless mistakes in his schoolwork. He tended not to finish the work he started in the classroom and he seemed to be easily distracted at his desk when the others appeared to be working. However, he did not seem hyperactive, he seemed to be able to wait his turn in games and other activities, and he didn't interrupt others or intrude on their activities.

I asked about Neil's ability to concentrate on activities he enjoyed. Neil said that he loved reading books about dinosaurs. I asked his mother how long Neil could sit quietly and read one of his books, and she said that he could sit and read for hours. I asked about his behavior at social gatherings, in restaurants, at church, and was told that his behavior was excellent and that he showed no signs at all of hyperactivity or impulsivity in those settings. Neil also appeared to be able to get along well with others and had several good friends at school. His only difficulty appeared to be with his teacher and his schoolwork.

I asked Neil's mother about her pregnancy with Neil, as well as Neil's delivery. She said that the pregnancy had been uneventful, that she had not drunk alcohol or smoked during the pregnancy, and that Neil was born at term with a normal delivery, weighing seven-and-a-half pounds. Neil left the hospital at thirty-six hours, which was customary at that hospital. His development in the first year of life was normal, even slightly advanced. He was walking at eleven months, and his language development was actually ahead of that of his older sister. He was toilet trained at two and knew his numbers, colors, and letters before he started junior kindergarten.

At no time before Grade 2 had anyone ever mentioned to Mrs. Smith that Neil was unable to concentrate, was hyperactive, or showed any impulsive behavior. Neil was taking no medications for any chronic illness and was quite healthy, never having been hospitalized and having been treated only for the usual respiratory infections that otherwise healthy children regularly have. His physical examination was completely normal.

I asked Neil to do some reading for me, and was very surprised to find that he was reading at least three grade levels ahead of where he should be. His writing was legible and he had no difficulty getting his ideas on paper. His knowledge of mathematics was appropriate for his grade level.

At that point it was clear that Neil did not have ADHD. His inattentiveness and inability to complete his work in the class was simply the result of boredom. He was clearly extremely bright and needed more of a challenge than he was being given by his Grade 2 teacher. Together his parents and I discussed approaching the school about giving him more challenges in class.

Neil's diagnosis, like Sam's, was based on the *DSM-IV*. He did not show very many of the symptoms of inattention, and he had no symptoms of hyperactivity or impulsiveness. The problem had not been noticed before he was seven, and it was only a problem at school, not anywhere else. It was affecting his relationship with his teacher, but it was not affecting social relationships or his academic abilities.

In between the Sams and the Neils are a whole spectrum of children with different symptoms, and different diagnoses. Some children are "borderline": they display some of the symptoms some of the time, but their behavior is inconsistent. One child fidgets constantly, unless he is concentrating on something he enjoys, and then he can concentrate with no difficulty at all. Another daydreams and then writes amazingly detailed science fiction stories about the things he has been envisioning in his daydreams. A little girl I know is very impulsive, blurting out her opinions and rushing into new projects that she never finishes, but she has no other symptoms of ADHD.

Children come in all varieties of temperament and personality, and thank goodness for that. I've heard of children who are just a little different—a little more emotional, a little over-enthusiastic, a little bit dreamy—being rushed off to the doctor, who is expected to pronounce the verdict of ADHD. Not all differences are pathological. This is why I take the process of diagnosis very seriously and encourage you to take lots of time to observe the child's behavior and think about the interview questions carefully before you talk to a professional.

The big question: to medicate or not to medicate?

If your child has been diagnosed correctly as having ADHD, the next question you will face is what type of treatment is most appropriate. For parents, the biggest question is whether or not to treat the child using medication. There are three main drugs used to treat ADHD: methylphenidate (Ritalin), dextroamphetamine (Dexedrine), and pemoline (Cylert). These are all stimulants. In some cases, antidepressants have been used instead, but first we will look at the effects of stimulants.

Before you make the important decision to put a child on medication, you need the answers to the following questions.

- Does stimulant medication really help children whose attentional problems affect their behavior and schoolwork?
- If it works, how does it work? Does it just slow children down so that the teacher will have an easier time?
- Does stimulant medication help children with their schoolwork as well as their behavior?
- Will it improve the child's self-esteem?
- Will it help the child get on better with classmates, teachers, and family members?

- What are the short-term and long-term side effects of stimulant medication?
- Is the medication contraindicated for children with other disorders or who are on medication for other health problems?
- How long will the child have to take the medication?
- Will the child become dependent on the medication or addicted to other drugs?

To help you make up your mind, I will try to answer these questions using the best available information from current research.

Does stimulant medication really help children with ADHD?

The first study of the effects of stimulants on hyperactive children was done in 1937, when Dr. Charles Bradley, an American doctor, used Benzedrine, a central nervous system stimulant, to treat children who had become hyperactive following a bout of viral encephalitis. He found that stimulants made the children less distractible and overactive. He reported his results, and soon other doctors started to use stimulants to treat children suffering from what was then called "hyperkinesis" or "minimal brain dysfunction." In 1959, doctors began to use methylphenidate (Ritalin) and it eventually became the preferred treatment for hyperactivity.

Since Bradley's discovery in 1937, more than 100 controlled clinical trials have been conducted on the effects of stimulant medications like Ritalin and Dexedrine on children with ADHD. Most of the studies have been randomized double-blind controlled trials. This means that, during the studies, the teachers, parents, children, and observers did not know which children were receiving medication and which were receiving placebos.

As I explained in Chapter 1, double-blind studies are designed to screen out the human tendency to see what we want to see. Many people have strong feelings about using medication on children. For example, a teacher who was strongly in favor of using medication to help children with ADHD might overstate any improvements in a child's behavior if he or she knew which child was receiving the medication. On the other hand, a teacher who felt that children with behavior problems should be given counseling and remedial instruction instead of medication might understate any improvements in the same situation.

Controlled studies have found that about 80 percent of children with ADHD benefit from medication in that their hyperactivity is reduced, and they become less distractible and impulsive, better able to focus their attention on schoolwork or some other activity. When doses are carefully adjusted and a different stimulant medication is used if the first one doesn't work, researchers have found that the proportion of children with ADHD who benefit is between 85 and 90 percent.

How does the medication work? Does it just slow children down?

Ritalin, Dexedrine, and Cylert are stimulants, not sedatives. Sedatives would slow children down, but they would also make them so sleepy that they would be unable to pay attention and keep up in school.

At first glance, it seems completely illogical to treat hyperactivity with stimulants. However, in low doses, stimulants enhance attention, which in turn suppresses overactivity. They help children focus and concentrate. They may improve children's moods and make them less aggressive. The children usually become calmer, and are in a better frame of mind to do schoolwork.

Exactly how stimulants create these effects is not fully understood. Stimulants are non-specific medications, which means that they act on different areas of brain function all at once. Among other things, they stimulate the production of neurotransmitters that send messages to various parts of the brain, including the areas that regulate activity and inhibit the need to respond to every single stimulus in the environment. When the self-regulatory part of the brain is functioning normally, children are better able to concentrate, screen out distractions, and control their movements.

Does the medication help children with their schoolwork as well as their behavior?

Medication can help children do better at school by reducing their restlessness and increasing their attention span. This makes it easier for children to read and study, listen to and learn from teachers, complete homework and other assignments, and focus on tests and examinations. However, if the child has a specific learning disability as well as ADHD, then medication alone will not help the child who is struggling with reading or math; remedial teaching will be necessary.

There are two kinds of research into the benefits of medication for ADHD. One type studies short-term changes in children's behavior and responses under laboratory conditions. The other studies the long-term changes in the regular classroom for children who are taking ADHD medication.

Results from these studies vary with the design of the study. The best designed short-term studies have generally had the most positive results; that is, they have found that children who take medication for ADHD do better at schoolwork than they would without medication. Others have had less clear results for a number of reasons:

- they have lumped together children with differing conditions, including hyperactive children who suffer from global developmental delays and those with specific learning disorders;
- they have tested the children using the Wide Range Achievement Test or the Wechsler Intelligence Scale for Children, which do not pick up on short-term changes in the children's achievements;
- they gave all the children the same dose of medication rather than trying to determine the best possible dose for each child.

However, studies such as that by Josephine Elia and her colleagues in Philadelphia evaluated children's school performance using measures such as the number of assignments completed, the number completed correctly, and specific tests of math and reading, and adjusted the dosage for each child. In these studies, the short-term improvement in schoolwork for children with ADHD who are receiving appropriate medication was clear.

A longer-term study conducted by researchers in Sweden tracked children with ADHD for fifteen months. The randomized, controlled, double-blind study looked at sixty-two children, of whom two-thirds had ADHD only and the other third had an additional problem or disorder in addition to ADHD. The researchers used the Wechsler Intelligence Scale for Children, which measures long-term academic gains. The study found clear improvements in the school achievement of the children who were taking medication for ADHD.

Will medication improve the child's self-esteem?

Yes, it will, given time. A randomized, double-blind controlled trial conducted by researchers in Texas used two measures of self-esteem: general self-esteem, or what the children thought of themselves as people, and academic self-esteem, or what the children thought of their ability to handle schoolwork. The study divided the children into two groups and gave the children in one group stimulant medication and those in the other group a placebo. The children were tested after one month on the medication, and again after sixteen months. There was no difference in their self-esteem after one month, but after sixteen months the differences were noticeable. The children who received the medication felt better about themselves and about their schoolwork.

Will the medication help the child get on better with other people?

Randomized controlled trials have even been able to demonstrate an improvement in these areas. In one study by researchers at McMaster University's Medical School, children who were receiving treatment for ADHD were less hyperactive, better able to stick with assigned tasks, and even better able to assume leadership. As their behavior improved, so did the attitudes of their classmates, who found them easier to get along with.

In another double-blind study at the University of California, researchers looked at the attitudes of teachers toward children with ADHD. The teachers became less intense and controlling toward children with ADHD who were receiving medication and whose behavior had improved. In effect, the teachers began to treat them just like the other, non-ADHD children in the classroom, and less like "problem" children.

Randomized controlled studies have even looked at family relationships. In a research study carried out by Russell Barkley and Charles Cunningham, the researchers noticed a change in the attitude of the mother toward the child once the child's behavior improved as a result of treatment. The mother was more likely to praise and reward the child and less likely to nag or scold.

Clearly, it seems that stimulant medication really can help many children with ADHD. Not all children respond to the medication—about 10 to 15 percent of those treated do not seem to experience the same improvements in their behavior and activity levels—but life for the children who do respond is much improved in terms of schoolwork, self-esteem, and relationships. However, do those benefits outweigh the drawbacks of taking medication?

What are the short-term and long-term side effects of stimulant medication?

The most common short-term side effects are personality changes, a reduced appetite, sleep disruptions, stomach ache, and headache. Most of these side effects disappear after a few weeks, but some of them may persist and may require a change in the timing, dosage, or type of medication. You should also be prepared for rebound effects, which are changes that occur as the medication wears off.

Personality changes

Some parents are unnerved when an energetic, bubbly, outgoing child starts taking the medication and becomes quiet, attentive, and subdued. They take the child off the medication even before they find out if this effect is temporary. It's an understandable reaction. The change can be very sudden and it may seem that the child is unhappy, compared with his previously noisy self. However, in most cases, the child will adjust once his body becomes more accustomed to the medication. He will be less rambunctious, naturally, but if he is customarily cheerful and friendly, this part of his personality will usually reassert itself, although in a calmer way. At the same time, his daydreaming, irritability, anxiety, and nail-biting will also decrease.

If the child seems lethargic, and complains of feeling over-tired or depressed, it may be that the dose is too high. Unlike many medications, the dose for Ritalin and other stimulants does not depend on the child's body weight, but on how quickly an individual metabolizes the drug. A dose that produces no discernible effect in one sixty-pound child may make another sixty-pound child glassy-eyed and apathetic. Talk to your doctor, who may recommend reducing the dose or changing to a different type of medication.

Another indication that the dose is too large is that the child, rather than becoming too quiet, becomes even more irritable or emotional and bursts into tears over small things. If you notice this reaction, talk to your doctor about reducing the dosage.

If your child is simply quieter than usual and it is you who are having difficulty accepting the change in behavior, give yourself and the child a few weeks to adjust. Try not to give up too soon.

Reduced appetite

This side effect may be temporary, or it may last as long as the child takes the medication. If the problem persists, there are a number of ways you can counteract this effect.

If the child takes the medication only during school hours, in the morning and at midday, then he or she will probably eat enough at breakfast, during the evenings, on weekends, and during school holidays to compensate for the lack of appetite during the day at school. His or her weight and height will not be affected. Make sure the child eats a good breakfast before taking the morning dose, and get the child to take the midday dose after lunch, not before. The medication will work whether the child takes it on a full or an empty stomach. You can also offer the child a nutritious bedtime snack with high-calorie, protein-rich foods such as milk, cheese, peanut butter, yogurt, or ice cream.

If the child takes the medication three times a day—morning, midday, and late afternoon—then, in addition to a good breakfast, a late afternoon snack before the third dose will also help. You may also find that, although the child is uninterested in large meals, he or she may be able to eat small snacks throughout the day that include protein-rich foods. You can also get nutrients into a child in the form of shakes, smoothies, and other high-protein drinks.

Even if the child is supposed to take the medication seven days a week, you can always skip a few doses on weekends so that he or she can eat larger meals then. It is not essential for the blood level of the medication to be constant at all times. Some children take the medication only during the school term and not at all during the summer vacation. A "drug vacation" from time to time is a good idea, unless the child's behavior is very difficult without the medication.

All children who are receiving medication for ADHD should be seen by the doctor who prescribed the medication every few weeks for the first few months of the treatment. The doctor will weigh the child, and note any significant loss of weight. If necessary, the doctor can adjust the dose or the type of medication, or the timing of the doses. If the child is already overweight, you may decide to wait and see before making changes.

Do not worry about stunting the child's growth. A long-term study on the effects of ADHD medication by Mortimer Gross of the University of Illinois showed that there is no difference in growth between children who are receiving treatment for ADHD and those who are not. Make sure the child eats nutritious meals as often as possible and allow for periods when the child does not take the medication. When the child stops taking the medication, his or her appetite will return immediately.

Sleep disruptions

Children who take ADHD medication in the late afternoon may have difficulty falling asleep at night. This effect usually disappears in time, so give it a few weeks before you consider making changes.

If the problem does not disappear, you need to determine whether it is the medication that is keeping the child awake or the lack of medication that is having this effect. Both are possible. The only way to find out is by experimenting. One weekend, try giving the child a dose in the evening. If the child falls asleep, then it is the lack of medication that is keeping him awake and he may need a regular evening dose. If, however, an evening dose makes the child wakeful, you should talk to your doctor about decreasing or skipping the late-afternoon dose, or changing to a different medication, or occasionally using an antihistamine (*not* a sleeping pill) to help him drop off to sleep.

Stomach aches, headaches

These effects are usually temporary as the body adjusts to the medication. A child who gets a headache immediately after taking the medication is probably taking too large a dose, and you should ask the doctor to change the dosage. If the headaches or stomach aches persist, talk to your doctor about changing the type of medication.

Rebound effects

Most ADHD medications remain in the bloodstream for about four hours on average, although in some children the effects may persist for five hours, or wear off after three hours. In some children, when the medication starts to wear off, they do not revert to their usual level of activity, but become even more hyperactive than they were before they took the medication. They may have tantrums or get angry easily, or become very excitable. These effects may last from forty-five minutes to an hour after the medication wears off.

If the medication is not causing sleep problems, then the answer may be to give the child another small dose that will take her through until bedtime. If the medication does interfere with the child's sleep, then it might be better to decrease the final dose of the day. In either case, discuss the rebound effect with your doctor before making any changes in dosage.

Is the medication contraindicated for certain children?

There are few contraindications for stimulant medications like Ritalin. Medication is rarely prescribed for children of five and under. Before a child begins any course of medication, the doctor should take a complete family history and do a complete physical checkup, including testing the child's blood pressure, and take a thorough family history. There are very few children who cannot undergo a trial of medication.

How long will the child have to take the medication?

It used to be thought that children would "outgrow" the need for stimulants in adolescence. However, as doctors and researchers continue to learn more about drugs like Ritalin, they are finding that at least half of the children with ADHD will still need stimulants in high school, if they are to continue making academic progress. Fewer than half, maybe as few as 10 percent, will probably need medication as adults.

The basis for these projections are studies such as one done in Baltimore County by Daniel Safer and John Krager. In Baltimore County, school nurses are regularly surveyed about the numbers of children receiving medication for ADHD. In 1975, the nurses reported that about 11 percent of those taking medication were in high school. In the 1990s, that figure had increased to 30 percent. Moreover, in recent surveys, the researchers found that 97 percent of the middle-school children (average age thirteen) who were taking medication for ADHD had been doing so for about five years.

Psychiatrists are also treating adult ADHD patients with stimulants and finding that they respond as well as elementary- and high-school students to the medication.

Nevertheless, some children seem to need medication less and less as time passes. At present it is not possible to predict which children will respond this way. The only way to tell if a child still needs medication is to do a single-blind test once a year. Choose a week in which there are no important tests or deadlines, but a week that is far enough into the school year to ensure that the teacher knows the child well. Without telling the teacher in advance (the teacher is the "blinded" observer in this experiment), stop giving the child medication.

If the child still needs medication, the teacher will notice a difference in the child's behavior within a day or so. The teacher may call you, but if not, call after a few days and ask how your child is doing without explaining why you are asking. The teacher may say that your child has been behaving well all year, but has been more disruptive and inattentive in the past few days. At this point, you can explain that you have taken the child off medication temporarily. However, if the teacher has not noticed any change in the child's behavior, and feels that the child is doing fine, it may be that your child no longer needs stimulants and can manage without them.

Will the child become dependent on the medication or addicted to other drugs?

Many parents and teachers disapprove of giving a child medication over the course of several years, believing that this will cause drug dependency and may lead to other addictions in later life. Long-term studies, such as that by Lily Hechtman at the Montreal Children's Hospital, have found, however, that children with ADHD who are treated with medication are no more likely to have drug or alcohol problems than other children. In fact, since impulsive, even dangerous behavior is one of the characteristics of untreated ADHD, it could well be that children who do not take medication to control ADHD are more likely to experiment with drugs or alcohol or glue-sniffing during adolescence, because they are less likely to think of long-term consequences before they act. I wouldn't go so far as to say that taking stimulant medication for ADHD *prevents* drug abuse later in life, but by improving a child's ability to control his or her actions, it may help adolescents resist temptations and peer pressure to some extent.

Nevertheless, there are several books that strongly oppose the use of stimulant medication for children with ADHD, claiming that the increase in the use of Ritalin and other drugs is the result of a dangerous "conspiracy" by drug companies and managed health-care organizations to increase their profits at the expense of unsuspecting children and families. These books often overstate the increase in stimulant medication prescriptions and the total number of children receiving the medication. Their claims about the long-term effects of the medication ignore the evidence of scientific studies. They often blame parents and teachers for children's emotional problems and recommend better parenting with stiffer discipline and more rigorous teaching methods as the "treatment" for ADHD.

You may also have heard about a group called Citizens' Commission on Human Rights, which strongly opposes the use of drugs like Ritalin, claiming that it is addictive and that its use increases the risk of later drug abuse. You should know that this group is funded by the Church of Scientology, which routinely opposes most psychiatric practices. The commission's claims are based on its political agenda, not on research. Scientology claims to treat a host of psychological disorders, and the church tends to oppose all forms of mainstream psychiatry.

No matter how often scientists publish the evidence that stimulant medication for ADHD does not lead to later drug abuse, the misinformation does not disappear. You will see it in newspapers and magazines and hear it on television and radio programs. You must be the judge. Talk to your doctor, get in touch with the organizations that represent people with ADHD, read some of the papers I have listed at the back of this book. The scientific research does not support the argument that stimulant medication is harmful for children in the long term.

Of course, stimulants should never be used by children other than to treat clinically diagnosed ADHD. You must be very careful with any supplies of the medication. Keep them locked up, and make sure that other family members, relatives, or friends do not have access to them. The only person taking the medication should be the child for whom it was prescribed. Stimulant abuse by young people does occur, and you have a responsibility to make sure that any drugs administered under your supervision are not lost or stolen.

Making the decision on medication

The research shows that stimulants can help many children with ADHD, although some children do not respond to the medication, for reasons that cannot be identified at present. For most children, as well as for their parents and teachers, the benefits of Ritalin or Dexedrine far outweigh any drawbacks. Quite often, the worse the behavior without medication, the more dramatic and positive the change with the medication.

Perhaps the last questions you need to answer before you make the decision should be questions about the individual child:

- Is his self-esteem suffering? Does he think of himself as an outcast or a troublemaker?
- Is she constantly in trouble at school because of disruptive behavior?
- Is he at risk of failing a grade because he can't pay attention in class?
- Is she having trouble making friends and feeling socially isolated?
- Is his behavior so impulsive that he is a danger to himself or others? (For example, does he run into the street without watching for traffic?)

- Is her behavior causing conflict within the family?
- Have you tried other forms of treatment that haven't worked?

If you do decide to give a child stimulants, be prepared for side effects at first. Most will disappear after a few weeks. Keep in touch with your doctor, so that you can adjust the quantity and timing of doses as well as the type of drug if necessary, and discuss the best times to skip a dose or two.

When you discuss any medication with the doctor, make sure you understand clearly what is required. Take a notepad to the appointment and make notes. Ask for a fact sheet to take away. Don't leave until you have the answers to the following questions:

- What is the recommended dose?
- How often and when should it be given?
- What are the possible side effects?
- Are there any foods that the child should avoid while taking the medication?
- If the child is taking other medications, will it react with them?
- If the child accidentally takes too much medication, what do we do?
- How often should we schedule further appointments for re-evaluation?

You should also be prepared for criticism of your decision. Some people say that Ritalin is overprescribed because parents and teachers are lazy, and administering a drug is easier than working to modify the child's behavior. This comment is unfair. Stimulants make life easier for the child, not the parents, and the child's interests should come first in all decision making about medication. Even when the child is taking medication, parents and teachers must still work closely with the child to help the child learn new habits and succeed at school. The difference is that, once the child is able to focus, the work of parents and teachers can be more constructive, rather than simply a struggle for control.

Opponents of stimulants also suggest that medicating a child just makes the child feel there is something wrong with him or her. It's a strange criticism, considering that children with untreated ADHD already feel that there is something wrong when they cannot make friends or succeed at school. When a child is already socially isolated because of the disorder, how could using medication make things worse?

Finally, as I have explained, critics of Ritalin state that the drug has the same effect as cocaine or speed and that in giving the drug to a child, you are paving the way for later drug abuse. They claim that no one knows the long-term effects of the drug. This is nonsense. Ritalin has been used safely for almost forty years and there have been numerous long-term studies on its effects. There is no evidence that it leads to drug abuse in later life, although there is evidence to suggest that some drug abusers do suffer from untreated ADHD.

Getting started with stimulant medication

Remember Sam, the little boy who was failing Grade 3? I recommended Ritalin, and his parents agreed to try it. I also asked to talk to Sam's teacher about the medication. I told her that Sam would be taking the medication, but I did not say when the treatment would begin or how long it would continue. I asked her to keep an eye on him, and note changes in his behavior, schoolwork, and relationships with other children. I explained that the reason I was not going to tell her when Sam would be receiving the medication was because I wanted her observations to be unbiased by this knowledge.

Sam did not get Ritalin for the first week after this conversation. The teacher told me that his behavior was essentially the same as usual. Sam received Ritalin the second week and the teacher noticed a change immediately. He was able to concentrate better, he seemed to listen more, and he wasn't so annoying to other children. At this point, we all agreed that Sam benefited from Ritalin and should continue.

Over the next few months, we made some adjustments to the dosage and the timing of the doses. He settled down at school and his work began to improve. The teacher encouraged his progress and kept in close touch with the parents about how he was doing. Gradually, the other children realized that he was easier to get on with and they stopped shutting him out. Although he didn't immediately develop close friendships, he was less of an outcast, and began to feel better about himself. He passed Grade 3 and began to enjoy school. Sam's improvement impressed his parents, and his father asked whether or not he could benefit from Ritalin. I suggested that he discuss the possibility fully with his own doctor.

Alternatives to stimulants

Some children with ADHD do not respond to stimulant medication, or they have so many problems with side effects that they cannot remain on the medication. Other children may suffer from depression as well as ADHD. For these children, doctors may recommend drugs called "tricyclic antidepressants." These drugs may also be recommended for teenagers and adults who have ADHD. They include imipramine (Tofranil), amitriptyline (Elavil), and desipramine (Norpramin).

Antidepressants work very differently from stimulants. For one thing, they remain in the body for much longer, unlike stimulants, which are usually completely metabolized in four to five hours. Antidepressants stay in the body for about twelve hours, so they are usually taken only twice a day. For another, they may not treat all three major symptoms of ADHD. Tofranil, for example, can help with hyperactivity and distractibility, but may not help with impulsiveness.

The beneficial effects of antidepressants, if any, take longer to appear, and the medication may also lose its effectiveness over time. Antidepressants should be taken regularly, unlike Ritalin, which can be stopped and started at any time. Missing a dose of an antidepressant can cause headaches, nausea, or aching muscles. If you decide to take the child off the medication, you should taper off, rather than simply stopping, in order to avoid these symptoms.

Antidepressants also have different side effects, including fatigue or sleepiness, constipation, dry mouth, or blurred vision. Certain antidepressants can slow down the heart rate and may increase the risk of seizures or convulsions. They may be contraindicated for children with a family history of heart problems or those who suffer from any kind of seizure disorder, such as epilepsy.

Fluoxetine (Prozac), one of a group of drugs known as selective serotonin reuptake inhibitors, has occasionally been suggested as a way to treat children with ADHD. Prozac is a fairly new drug, and its effects on children have not been fully studied. It may make aggressive or hyperactive children calmer, and it may improve impulse control, although its effect on attention span are less noticeable than the effects of stimulant medication. Unlike other antidepressants, it does not slow the heart rate, but it may produce other side effects, such as anxiety or nervousness, which is the exact opposite of the desired effect. It may also cause nausea, headaches, or insomnia. Until more study has been done on the use of Prozac for ADHD, I would not recommend its use.

In some cases, a doctor may recommend a combination of stimulants and antidepressants. At present, there are few controlled studies on the benefits and potential side effects of this approach, and the recommendation should be treated with extreme caution. You may want to get a second opinion before administering any kind of "drug cocktail" to a child. Each of the drugs I have described has a very different effect on different individuals, and therefore possible drug interactions are impossible to predict with certainty.

Finally, clonidine (Catapres), a medication called an "antihypertensive" that is usually used to treat high blood pressure in adults, has been suggested as a way to treat children with ADHD. I do not recommend this drug. There is little research that supports its effectiveness, and the side effects include headaches, dizziness, lowered blood pressure, nausea, changes in appetite or sleep patterns, and occasionally anxiety.

Whatever your doctor recommends, be prepared to ask a lot of questions before you give the medication to your child, and make sure that the doctor sees the child regularly, so that you can discuss any problems or side effects.

Using behavior modification to help children with ADHD

Behavior modification, also known as "behavior management," is one of those ideas that sounds very simple but can be very difficult to put into practice. The notion of rewarding good behavior and punishing or stopping bad behavior is straightforward. Most parents do this anyway. We praise our children when they behave well, encouraging them to continue to do this kind of behavior. When they don't behave well, we express our anger or disappointment, and we may take away certain privileges to remind them not to misbehave again.

So far, so good. But children are not performing animals who can be trained with carrots and sticks, and their reactions to praise or anger are not always predictable. For example, if their parents seem to pay more attention to bad behavior than to good behavior, children may behave badly on purpose, because they know it will get them the attention they want. If they behave well, their parents may not notice them as much. Sometimes making an adult angry gives a child a sense of power: "I must be a pretty powerful person if I can get that important adult in my life so upset."

Clearly, there's more to behavior modification than praising or punishing. Therefore, it's more helpful to think in terms of reinforcement or extinction. Reinforcement is anything that makes a child likely to repeat a certain kind of behavior, good or bad. Good behavior can be reinforced with praise or a hug, or a tangible reward like a sticker or cookie. Bad behavior can also be reinforced with something else the child wants: an excited reaction from an adult or a disruption in routine.

Extinction is the opposite of reinforcement. It is whatever makes a child unlikely to repeat an action. Ignoring a child's efforts to succeed or to please will make the child less enthusiastic about making the same effort in future. On the other hand, ignoring a child's deliberately naughty behavior, provided it is not causing significant problems for other people, may make the child feel that it is pointless to persist.

Most authorities on behavior management recommend reinforcement for good behavior and extinction for bad behavior, and punishment only for behavior that is dangerous. Punishment usually involves taking away a privilege ("That's it, no television tonight"), or adding an extra chore ("You're not going anywhere until you clean up this mess"). As for spanking, most school systems have made corporal punishment illegal, and most child-care experts recommend that parents avoid it as well. Although there is no clear evidence that a child who is occasionally spanked for misbehavior will develop long-term problems as a result, there is also no evidence that spanking is a particularly effective or appropriate punishment in terms of behavior modification. There are better ways to get your message across to a child.

Using behavior management to help children with ADHD

There are three important elements of successful behavior management:

- Let the child know what to expect ahead of time. The child and the adult need to share an understanding about what behaviors are acceptable, what are unacceptable, and what the consequences of each kind of behavior will be.
- Make sure any reinforcement or reward is meaningful. This means that the reward must be something the child really wants and is willing to work for. Also, since children with ADHD have short attention spans, the rewards should be small and frequent, rather than large and infrequent. Promising a child a bicycle at the end of term if he or she has a good report card will not work as well as offering small daily or weekly inducements to behave.
- Stick with your agreement. Behavior modification won't work if you only remember to do it once a week. It won't work if one parent uses it and the other doesn't. Reinforcement must be consistent, so that the child always knows where he or she stands.

At school, the teacher can draw up a formal agreement with a child and the child's parents. The agreement should specify what behavior the teacher expects, and how the child will be rewarded if he or she behaves that way. For example, for every hour that the child is attentive and not disruptive in class, he or she will get a gold star or sticker, and for every day that the child gets a certain number of stickers, he or she will get some meaningful reward at home, such as a special dessert after dinner, or time spent playing a favorite game with a parent. Additional rewards can be offered for completing certain tasks or improving performance on assignments and tests.

The extinction of negative behavior is just the opposite of reinforcing the good behavior: the child fails to get the star or sticker and thereby must forfeit the reward that goes with it. Otherwise, bad behavior is ignored, rather than reinforced with the teacher's attention, unless the behavior harms other children or disrupts the whole class. Some kind of penalty for these behaviors should be included in the agreement, so that the child knows exactly what to expect if he or she hits another child or prevents another child from working.

A similar approach can also work in the home, with a scoring system for evidence of good behavior, such as being on time for meals, carrying out daily chores without nagging, tidying up a room or play area, finishing homework, or going to bed when told to do so. When the child achieves a certain score within a certain time period, then he or she is eligible for a reward. When the child fails to behave, the rewards are withdrawn. For extremely bad behavior, regular privileges are revoked. Television time may be cut back, an outing may be canceled, or pocket money may be reduced.

Behavior-modification experts also recommend using "time out" as a form of correcting bad behavior. When the child behaves unacceptably, he or she is isolated from the rest of the family in a different room for a specified time, such as twenty minutes. The length of time depends on the child's age: ten minutes is probably enough for a small child, but an hour may be appropriate for a teenager. Some parents use a timer, and if the child comes out before the time is up, or continues to misbehave, the timer is reset. The time out is for cooling off, which may be necessary for both the child and the parent. As with all forms of behavior management, you should let the child know up front what to expect, "If you hit your brother, I will send you to your room for half an hour. No exceptions." Time out should be the known consequence of certain kinds of behavior.

Over time, any behavior-modification program will have to be adjusted. Certain rewards may lose their attraction for the child. Or the child may correct one type of problem behavior only to develop a new one. It is a good idea to start by focusing on a few specific areas (not interrupting the teacher in class, staying in seat) and getting the child into some new habits, before introducing incentives to improve in other areas (completing assignments and tests).

The pros and cons of behavior management

As I mentioned earlier, it is a fairly simple matter to design a behavior-modification program. Carrying it out is the tricky part. Behavior modification is labor-intensive, and requires constant vigilance. Parents and teachers have many demands on their time, and they cannot monitor a single child constantly.

One problem is that real-life situations are never as clearcut as they are in the textbooks. According to the textbooks, one should be able to say calmly to a child who has just told her brother that he's a moron and she hates him, "Now, Susie, that wasn't a very nice thing to say to Billy and you won't get your gold star for this evening." In real life, these events never happen in isolation, at a time when you can assess them carefully and come up with an appropriate response. They happen when dinner preparations have reached a critical stage, the television is on, the phone is ringing, and another child is trying to get your attention about a problem with his math homework. You hear the children quarreling in the distance, but you can't be sure exactly what was said, and you don't have a moment to take them aside and sort it out. You can't provide immediate feedback on every domestic event.

The other problem is that behavior modification requires considerable self-control on the part of the parent or teacher. Parents and teachers get tired or ill, they have emotional upheavals in their lives, and they may sometimes find it difficult to respond with the kind of dispassionate evaluation that the behavior-modification experts recommend. It's one thing for a textbook writer to say, "Don't let your mood affect your reaction to your child's behavior," it's another thing to exercise the necessary self-control when your child is standing in the middle of the department store, screaming, it's the week before Christmas, and you are overwhelmed with social and work obligations and feeling at your wits' end.

I'm not saying these things to discourage you from setting up a behavior-modification program, but I do want to prepare you for the effort involved in sticking to one.

Not all parents like the idea of behavior modification. Some find the whole idea unnatural, too manipulative. Although most parents instinctively practice an informal type of behavior modification, elaborate programs with stars and rewards and lists and charts are not for everybody. As one mother put it, "It becomes too much a matter of scoring points, almost an end in itself." If the goal of behavior modification—a long-term improvement in the child's behavior—gets lost in the day-to-day battle of wills between parent and child, it may be time to rethink the approach.

Other parents object to the idea of material rewards for

good behavior. They feel it is too close to bribing children. They worry that, after experiencing formal behavior modification, children will never learn to behave well without the inducements and will go through life expecting some kind of material reward for good behavior. They consider the use of material rewards a short-term solution for immediate problems, rather than a long-term strategy for improving behavior. There is no evidence one way or the other to suggest that behavior modification does long-term harm, but if the idea of material rewards makes you uncomfortable, make the rewards social instead. Instead of offering a new toy, offer an hour of your own time to play a game that the child enjoys.

Some parents object to certain recommendations made by behavior-modification experts. Some of them seem very harsh. For example, one writer recommends a "refusal to parent" if the child refuses to behave acceptably. He suggests not talking to the child, not setting a place at the table for the child, not interacting in any way. This goes beyond simply ignoring bad behavior and sounds uncomfortably like the Amish practice of "shunning," whereby a recalcitrant member of the community is treated as if he or she did not exist. I personally find this too extreme, and I do not know of many parents who are cold and calculating enough to carry it off.

If you plan to use behavior modification, you must come up with a program that you can live with, that doesn't require you to act in ways that make you feel uncomfortable. It should also be one that is not so complicated that you abandon it after the first week. Keep the agreement simple, set realistic goals, decide on appropriate reinforcements, make any punishments reasonable.

If you do stick with it, a behavior-modification program may be as good for you as it is for the child:

- It forces you to be more aware of your own reactions and your own attitudes. It can help you, as a parent or teacher, identify times when your reaction to the child is reinforcing the child's bad behavior instead of extinguishing it.
- It means making a habit of praising the child whenever he or she behaves well, which is a good habit to get into.
- It involves planning, as you learn to predict the situations that trigger bad behavior and plan around them. This is another good habit to get into.
- It requires you to be calm and constructive in difficult situations, to count to ten and take a deep breath before speaking, and not to give in to knee-jerk reactions.

Altogether, not a bad crash course in parenting or teaching skills.

Does behavior modification really improve the behavior of children with ADHD?

Although there have been many randomized controlled trials that show that the benefits of stimulant medication outweigh the drawbacks for most children with ADHD, there is much less evidence for the effectiveness of behavior modification.

Nevertheless, there are a few studies that have tried to test this approach. One study, conducted by Howard Abikoff and Rachel Gittelman, looked at children with ADHD who were not receiving medication. Their teachers and parents were taught behavior-management techniques by trained therapists. The rewards included money, television time, treats, or special time with a parent. Twenty-eight children with ADHD were subject to behavior modification, and twenty-eight children who did not have ADHD did not receive any special treatment and served as controls. The children's behavior was monitored every thirty minutes, so that they would get frequent feedback. "Blinded" observers, who did not know which children were being treated, sat in the classroom and reported on the children's behavior. The goal of the study was to find out if eight weeks of intense behavior modification at home and in school would lead to a measurable improvement in the children's behavior.

After eight weeks there was some improvement in aggressive behavior, but no discernible change in the children's impulsiveness, attention, or activity levels. Admittedly, the sample size was small, and it was not a randomized controlled trial, but still, the results of such intensive behavior therapy were not encouraging.

In another study, by researchers in Ottawa, children with ADHD and their families were randomly assigned to one of three groups:

- Group 1 parents were trained in behavior modification and the children were given a placebo pill.
- Group 2 parents were trained in behavior modification and the children were given methylphenidate (Ritalin).
- Group 3 parents received no training and the children were given methylphenidate.

The children in Groups 2 and 3 did better academically than those in Group 1, and they also improved in terms of impulse control and attentiveness. There was no significant difference between the children in Groups 2 and 3. The methylphenidate seems to make the children behave better, even when the parents did not use behavior modification.

In another randomized controlled trial, the researchers increased the amount of behavior modification by providing it at school as well as at home. The results were similar. Behavior modification helps, but not as much as the stimulant medication.

Can behavior modification be used without also giving medication?

There are two situations in which I would recommend behavior modification without medication for children with ADHD.

First, I would suggest it in any case in which the diagnosis of ADHD is not clear. For example, a school may report that a child shows inattentive, impulsive behavior in the classroom, but the parents do not see evidence of this behavior at home. Or a child may sometimes display symptoms of ADHD, but not often enough for the diagnosis to be certain.

Second, I recommend behavior modification to parents who are strongly opposed to the use of medication for children or who want to try non-drug approaches before they consider medication.

Otherwise, if the diagnosis is clear and the parents are willing, I recommend that children be given medication, and the child's health and behavior be closely monitored for the first few months. During this time, the parents, teachers and I look for changes in attention, schoolwork, relationships, activity levels, and impulse control, and for any side effects that do not disappear within a few days.

If the child's behavior is clearly improving, then there is probably no need for a formal program of behavior modification. Parents and teachers are generally disposed to reward good behavior and ignore inappropriate behavior, as long as it is not dangerous to the child or other people. Once the child's behavior improves with medication, then the number of rewards are likely to increase and the number of instances of bad behavior will lessen. The child will get the reinforcement he or she needs without a formal behavior-modification program.

If, however, after adjustments to make sure the child is receiving the right drug in the right doses at the right times, the child's behavior is better but still causing some problems, I recommend that the parents and teachers consider practicing a more overt and conscious type of behavior modification. The medication will help the child benefit from behavior modification, because it allows him or her to block out distractions and remember: "If I do my work and don't interrupt the teacher too much, I'll get my gold stars, which I can cash in tonight when I get home."

Can social skills training improve the behavior of children with ADHD?

Many children with ADHD have difficulty forming good social relationships with other children. They may lack certain skills that seem to come naturally to other children, such as greeting people when they see them, chatting easily, smiling, and saying positive things about others. Researchers have found that social skills are not only a problem with other children, but also with teachers and parents.

Most children learn by experience that when they treat other people politely and kindly, they get equally pleasant treatment in response. They learn to be friendly because they enjoy having friends, and to be generally sociable because they want to be part of a group, not an outsider. Children with ADHD, however, may lack this ability to think ahead about the consequences of their behavior. They may say the first thing that comes into their heads when they meet someone, and it may not be complimentary. They may be distracted during a conversation and lose interest, which makes the person who is talking feel stupid. They may suddenly interrupt someone else, or walk off when something else catches their eye, which makes the other person feel rejected. Non-ADHD children don't have a lot of patience with this kind of behavior, and a child without social skills can quickly become a social outcast, able to associate only with other outcasts. Anger at being left out may lead them to behave badly just to get some attention. This is not true of all children with ADHD. Some are bubbly and funny and sought out by others. Others become the class clown, the kids who make everyone laugh, but who are constantly in trouble because the laughter of their classmates means more than the approval of their teachers or parents or the long-term goal of doing well at school.

Some schools have developed social-skills training to help children learn social skills if they do not seem to have acquired them on their own. The children watch videotapes of different situations, discuss the situations with other children, do role-playing exercises to practice social behavior, and play games that require interacting with others. The children work on the skills such as cooperation, communication, participation, and supporting others.

How useful are these training courses? John Coie and Gina Krehbiel at Duke University decided to find out. They worked with Grade 4 students who had academic and social problems. The children were randomly assigned to four groups:

- Group 1 received social-skills training only.
- Group 2 received academic skills training in the form of one-to-one tutoring in reading, math or both.
- Group 3 received both social and academic skills training.
- Group 4 was the control group and received no extra training.

The results were surprising. The children who did the best in both academic *and* social skills after six months of training were those in Group 2, the group that received academic training only. They did even better than Group 3, which received both academic and social-skills training.

Presumably the improvement in the Group 2 students came about because as their schoolwork improved, they got more positive feedback from teachers, which made them feel better about themselves. As the children began to participate more in the academic work in the classroom, their problem behaviors decreased. Their classmates noticed the change and the fact that the teacher was treating them with more respect. The classmates began to change their opinions about these children and act in a more friendly way.

Meanwhile, the children in Groups 1 and 3 did improve somewhat compared to those in Group 4. However, because the experiment did not include an attention-placebo group, it is hard to know whether the improvements occurred because of the type of training they received or just the extra attention. A study comparing a group that receives social-skills training and a group that gets an attention-placebo would be useful in showing whether social-skills training really does help children with ADHD or other learning difficulties.

Do children with ADHD benefit from special diets?

All kinds of special diets have been proposed to lessen the symptoms of ADHD. As I explained on pages 112–13, there is no evidence linking ADHD to diet, so I cannot recommend any of them. I do recommend that all children, whether or not they have ADHD, eat a healthy diet that draws on all the basic food groups, but I do not recommend eliminating any particular food from the diet. However, since you will no doubt hear about many of these diets, I will review the evidence for each one so you put the claim of diet proponents in perspective.

Sugar

For years, the idea that too much sugar in the diet causes hyperactivity and behavioral problems has been circulating. There is a certain intuitive logic to this thinking. Sugar provides a burst of energy, which is why many athletes and people who play sports eat high-carbohydrate snacks before competing or playing sports. If some sugar helps people stay active, perhaps extra sugar makes people overactive.

Unfortunately—or fortunately, depending on your point of view—the evidence shows that this thinking is false. Several randomized controlled trials have compared children with ADHD who were given a diet high in sugar to children with ADHD who received a placebo. The children were studied in the classroom by "blinded" observers who did not know which children were receiving the high-sugar or the low-sugar diet. The observers could not see a difference in the behavior of the two groups.

This type of study has been repeated by different people in different settings and the results are always the same. For example, one study, conducted in 1986 by Richard Milich and William Pelham, carefully examined twenty-five different aspects of behavior in young boys with ADHD, including academic performance, social behavior, rule violations, and body movements. Again, they found no differences between the boys who were given a diet with extra sugar and those who were on a low-sugar diet.

Most experts now accept that sugar is not the culprit in ADHD, but this idea has not been widely accepted by the general public. Many people still firmly believe that too much sugar causes hyperactivity. We've all heard about the "Twinkie defence," in the trial of Dan White for the murder of Harvey Milk, a civic official, in San Francisco in 1978. White claimed that he acted irrationally because he had eaten too much sugar in junk food. Despite widespread criticism of this junk-science defence, the judge accepted White's argument.

Many parents fully believe that their children become unmanageable when they eat too much sugar. "You should see him at Halloween; he's practically climbing the walls after eating the candy he gets." "Whenever she goes to a birthday party and eats all that cake, she's on such a sugar-high that you can't get a word in edgewise." In cases like these, the excitement of dressing up at Halloween or romping at a party with other children may be the real reason for the extra energy and activity.

Other parents see a connection between a particular food and their child's problem behavior. Particular types of candy or high-sugar snacks are blamed for everything from distractibility to aggressiveness. Daniel Hoover and Richard Milich once carried out a study on sugar consumption in which the mother was "blinded" about whether or not her child was eating sugar and found that, in general, mothers see what they expect to see. They expect extra activity after their child eats sugar; they look for it, and they invariably see it, whatever the child is doing. In the study, even when the children ate something sweet that contained artificial sweetener, not sugar, the mothers usually reported extra activity.

"Doctor, whenever she eats frosted cupcakes, she just goes wild." This kind of comment reminds me of that ancient joke. *Patient*: Doctor, every time I bend my arm this way, it hurts. *Doctor*: So don't bend your arm that way. If you as a parent truly believe that your child becomes a little monster when you give her frosted cupcakes, then stop giving her frosted cupcakes. You don't have to put the child on a special low-sugar diet, but I never discourage parents from introducing more healthful foods into a child's diet. You can substitute fruit for cake or peanut butter sandwiches for chocolate bars when your child is hungry. It won't make much difference to the child's behavior, but it may do wonders for her dental health.

The Feingold diet

I mentioned Dr. Benjamin Feingold on page 112. He asserted that additives, food coloring, and natural salicylates (the substance that gives many foods a sharp or tangy flavor) adversely affect a child's learning and attention. He recommended a diet that eliminates almonds, apples, apricots, berries, cherries, grapes, oranges, peaches, plums, tomatoes, cucumbers, luncheon meats, colored cheeses, most breads, cereals, baked goods, desserts, candy, artificially flavored beverages, mustard, ketchup, margarine, and colored butter. He also required followers of the diet to do without toothpaste, mouthwash, cough drops, antacids, vitamins, and most pediatric medications. It's a fairly extreme approach that would make most children very unhappy. One expert called it a "new form of child abuse."

The National Institutes of Health reviewed Feingold's work at a three-day conference of experts in 1982 and found that, although a few children (perhaps 1 percent of those studied) did respond positively to the diet for reasons that were not clear, in general the diet was not effective in treating ADHD. Further randomized controlled studies have supported this conclusion. Researchers found no difference between children with ADHD who were kept on this severe diet and those who were given a similar diet but one that did contain additives, food coloring, and salicylates. In 1986, Dr. Esther Wender reviewed studies that claimed to find a connection between additives and behavior. She found that most of them were seriously flawed and did not support Feingold's claims.

I certainly do not recommend that you remove fruits, breads, cereals, or other foods from your child's diet. For one thing, removing fruits from the child's diet could lead to a vitamin C deficiency. For another, it's an approach that is likely to increase domestic conflict rather than reduce it. Your child will feel singled out, unable to attend birthday parties or other events at which children eat together. You will find it increasingly difficult to construct healthy meals with such a limited range of acceptable foods. It's a recipe for family discord.

Allergen-free diets

In books such as *Is This Your Child? Discovering and Treating Unrecognized Allergies* (1992), Dr. Doris Rapp estimates that about three out of four people in the United States suffer from some type of allergy, or a sensitivity to certain foods or substances in the environment. She blames allergies not only for rashes and breathing problems, but also for fatigue, headaches, stomach problems, sleep problems, alcoholism, obesity, depression and suicide—and, of course, ADHD and learning problems.

Dr. Rapp's claims do not square with established medical science. She uses a testing method called provocation/neutralization that has been rejected by the American Academy of Allergy and Immunology. She opposes the use of Ritalin, describing it as addictive, which is untrue. She claims that her approach improves the behavior of children with ADHD, even though other researchers have been unable to duplicate these results.

Dr. Rapp recommends a diet that eliminates foods such as milk, chocolate, eggs, wheat, corn, peanuts, pork, and sugar, and then reintroduces them one at a time to test the effects on the child's behavior. There are no randomized controlled studies that support using this approach to treat children with

ADHD. No doctors or researchers have been able to get the same results that she claims to get with these methods.

Various organizations and centers have been created that claim to treat ADHD using elimination diets and other techniques for controlling allergies. For example, Mary Ann Block, an osteopath and author of *No More Ritalin: Treating ADHD without Drugs* (1996), offers a program of testing and seminars for children with ADHD and their parents at her center. Despite the glowing testimonials on her Web site and promotional literature, and exposure in the media for her story that she successfully treated her own daughter's health problems using the osteopathic approach, there is no scientific evidence that her treatment has any merit.

Dr. William Crook, a pediatrician and allergist who practices in Jackson, Tennessee, has proposed a slightly different theory in his self-published book *The Yeast Connection: A Medical Breakthrough* (1984). He has tried to connect hyperactivity with yeast infections and an allergy to yeast, which he calls "candidiasis hypersensitivity syndrome." Like Dr. Rapp, he ascribes a long list of health and psychiatric problems to yeast infections, from headaches and joint pain to anxiety, suicidal depression, and ADHD. He claims that treating the yeast infection will improve these problems.

The treatment he recommends is a diet low in sugar and additives, and a systematic elimination program similar to that proposed by Dr. Rapp, to identify foods that might cause an allergic reaction. He also recommends antifungal medication to combat the supposed yeast infection, and vitamin and mineral supplements.

Other than the vague claim that yeast infections "irritate the nervous system," Dr. Crook has never satisfactorily explained the connection between yeast and hyperactivity or attentional difficulties. There is no evidence to support his theories, and the

American Academy of Allergy and Immunology have issued a statement saying that his theories about candidiasis hypersensitivity syndrome are "speculative and unproven."

The diets suggested by Drs. Rapp and Crook will not help a child with ADHD. If the child has allergies, by all means go to your doctor for an assessment. However, once the respiratory and digestive problems caused by allergies and certain food sensitivities are brought under control, the ADHD will be unaffected and will still need treatment with medication, behavior modification, or both.

Megavitamin therapy

In 1977, Dr. Allan Cott published *The Orthomolecular Approach to Learning Difficulties*, claiming that learning disabilities and ADHD could be treated with massive doses of vitamins. Although he did not produce any research to support his theories, he based them on the use of megavitamins to treat schizophrenia, a since-discredited practice that was current at the time. His ideas also fitted in with the ideas of Nobel prize–winner Linus Pauling, who also recommended megavitamins for a variety of health and psychiatric problems.

It has long been known that vitamin deficiencies do cause health problems. Lack of vitamin C causes scurvy, and lack of vitamin D causes rickets, for example. However, there is no evidence to suggest that taking vitamins in quantities far in excess of the amount present in a normal healthy diet will cure illness or change behavior.

In one study by Dr. Robert Haslam and other researchers at the University of Calgary, forty-one children with ADHD were treated with megavitamins for three months. Their parents and teachers were aware that they were receiving the vitamin therapy. At the end of three months, the teachers and parents were surveyed about any changes in the children's behavior. The researchers then chose twelve children who were said to have benefited from the therapy. Over the next four months, these children received megavitamin therapy for six weeks, and then placebos for six weeks. This time, the researchers did not tell the parents and teachers when the children were receiving the supplements. According to the teachers' and parents' observations in the second half of the study, some of the children had more behavior problems during the therapy than during the times they were receiving the placebo.

Not only is it clear that megavitamins do not improve the behavior of children with ADHD, there is also considerable evidence that certain vitamins are toxic in large quantities and may do real harm. Excessive doses of vitamin A cause headaches, vomiting, diarrhea, rashes, blurred vision, and hair loss. Too much vitamin C can cause kidney stones. Vitamin D in large doses can lead to vomiting, weakness, anxiety, depression, extreme thirst, and calcium deposits in the kidneys, liver, and stomach.

Because of the potential problems of overdosing with megavitamins, do not try to treat a child with ADHD in this way.

Mineral supplements

The notion of treating children with mineral supplements is based on the theory that learning disorders and ADHD are caused by deficiencies of minerals. These minerals include chromium, copper, magnesium, manganese, and zinc, which are usually present in minute (trace) amounts in the body and minerals that are present in larger amounts, such as calcium, iron, and sodium. In recent years, attention has also focused on the trace elements iodine and selenium.

Proponents of these theories recommend measuring the amounts of these elements in a child's body by analyzing hair and nail clippings. If the levels of any of these elements are low, mineral supplements are recommended to replace them.

For example, Dr. Joel Wallach of California (he is not an M.D. but a veterinarian and a naturopathic doctor) offers a concoction of "colloidal minerals" that he calls "God's Recipe" or "The Natural Alternative to Ritalin." Most of the claims made on Dr. Wallach's Web site are either unverifiable or misleading (such as the claim that he was nominated for a Nobel prize). The products he sells are not subject to testing for either safety or effectiveness.

There are no randomized controlled trials that support the use of mineral supplements to treat ADHD. Even the method of testing by analyzing hair and nail clippings is unreliable, since substances in the environment may contaminate the samples, including trace elements in soaps or shampoos. Also, just as excessive doses of vitamins cause health problems, too much of certain minerals can do harm. For example, taking an overdose of iron causes abdominal pain and liver damage. Too much zinc can cause vomiting, fever, headaches, and abdominal pain.

Because of the potential for doing harm and the lack of evidence that mineral supplements actually help children with ADHD or learning disorders, you should avoid this approach.

Essential fatty acids (EFAs)

Certain fatty acids are the building blocks of cell membranes and prostaglandins, substances that play an important role in regulating many body functions such as blood pressure, temperature, and the movement of involuntary muscles.

A number of groups have suggested that lack of these essential fatty acids causes ADHD. Some early studies found lower levels of EFAs in children with ADHD than in children who do not have ADHD. However, these studies were not confirmed by later research.

A randomized controlled study was carried out by researchers in New Zealand. Children with ADHD were divided into two groups. One group was given capsules containing EFAs for four weeks and a placebo capsule for the next four weeks. The other group received the treatment in the reverse order. The children's parents and teachers did not know which children were in which group. The results of the study showed no difference between the behavior of the children who were receiving EFA supplements and those who were receiving the placebo.

Since EFA supplements are quite expensive and apparently make no difference to the behavior of children with ADHD, I do not recommend this approach.

Blue-green algae

John F. Taylor, author of *Helping Your Hyperactive ADD Child* (1997) and a proponent of the Feingold diet, has written a paper promoting blue-green algae as a nutritional supplement for children with ADHD. He claims that the algae contain amino acids, essential fatty acids, vitamins, and minerals and that these substances are essential in the treatment of ADHD. Not only are these claims without foundation, but some of the marketers of blue-green algae products have been served with legal injunctions by the U.S. government, requiring them to stop making therapeutic claims for these products. Despite the injunction, the algae supplements, which are very expensive, are still being sold on the Internet.

Blue-green algae is not only valueless as a nutritional supplement, it may even cause liver damage because of toxins called "microcystins" that occur naturally in the algae. Health Canada, through the Office of Natural Health Products, Therapeutic Products Program, and the Food Directorate of the Health Protection Branch, has undertaken a risk-assessment survey of products containing blue-green algae to determine the levels of microcystins they contain. Preliminary tests found several products containing blue-green algae with microcystin levels that exceeded those considered safe for daily consumption by the World Health Organization. Don't put your child's health at risk by trying to treat him or her with blue-green algae.

Food fads and diet myths

We North Americans seem to be obsessed with our weight, health, and appearance and we fall easy prey to food-faddists and diet promoters. Every year there are new "miracle" diets that promise to make us all slimmer, more energetic, less susceptible to the aging process, or more attractive. ADHD has come in for its fair share of attention from the people who sell diet books and nutritional supplements. Many of these unfounded ideas get media attention because the media loves stories of "miracle cures" and "medical breakthroughs." Proponents go on talk shows to tout their theories and products and late-night infomercials urge us to buy the latest wonder supplement.

The Internet is crammed with advertisements for nutritional supplements that claim to help children with ADHD. They have names like "Calm Focus" or "Attention Link," and the Web sites feature numerous testimonials from supposedly satisfied customers.

Be skeptical; be very skeptical. Medical researchers have performed countless experiments and studies, and there is not a shred of evidence to show that ADHD can be successfully treated with special diets or nutritional supplements. Let your common sense be your guide. Give your child a healthy balanced diet, and don't deprive your child of occasional treats.

Biofeedback

You may see advertisements that claim that a child with ADHD can be helped with biofeedback. The idea behind this claim is that, since ADHD is related to brain activity, biofeedback can help children exercise more control over their brain activity. In biofeedback, electrodes are attached to the child's scalp to detect brain waves. The information is displayed to the child, who then learns to do various exercises that alter the pattern of brain waves. Over time, the child supposedly acquires the ability to consciously alter negative patterns—that is, those associated with hyperactive, impulsive, or distractible behavior—and create more positive patterns, associated with concentration, focus, and calmer behavior.

The sessions are very expensive, and a great many sessions are necessary to achieve the desired result. No randomized controlled trials on the treatment have been done. The children who are supposed to have been helped with this therapy have also received other forms of treatment, so it is impossible to say which treatment caused the improvement. The organization Children and Adults with Attention Deficit Disorder (CHADD) convened a committee to review the literature on biofeedback. The group concluded that there was no evidence that the treatment is effective, or that the claims of its promoters are valid. Don't waste money on this dubious procedure.

Conduct disorder versus ADHD

Some doctors lump conduct disorder and attention deficit hyperactivity disorder together. This leads to rash generalizations, such as the statement "Jails are full of people with ADHD." People justify this opinion by pointing to the fact that children with conduct disorders also have ADHD, characterized by hyperactivity, impulsiveness, and inattention. However, they ignore the fact that the reverse is not true—that is, *most children with ADHD do not have conduct disorder.* If about 5 percent of the population has ADHD, then a much smaller percentage has conduct disorder—less than 1 percent.

I believe that the two conditions are quite separate, and that lumping the two together not only causes unnecessary confusion, but also unfairly stigmatizes children who have ADHD and only ADHD.

Conduct disorder is a serious, troubling condition that causes children and young people to be physically aggressive toward people and animals. They show little regard for the feelings, needs, or rights of others. Bullying, fighting, and threatening or scaring people are typical behaviors. They may even use weapons—a knife, a brick, a gun. When they are teenagers, they may force others into unwanted sex. Their aggressiveness is directed not only at people, but also at animals. Children with conduct disorder have been known to kick, hit, or stab family pets.

Conduct disorder also makes individuals destructive. They may set fires, or destroy someone else's property, smashing television sets or windows, breaking doors, or punching holes in walls. They grab what they want, either by shoplifting, stealing from family or friends, or forcing someone to give them something. Children with conduct disorder lie repeatedly to get what they want or to get out of doing something they don't want to do. They may repeatedly fail to show up at school and may even run away from home.

All children do some of these things now and again. Children lie occasionally, usually to stay out of trouble, teenagers cut classes once in a while, and some children even run away from home. Young people with conduct disorder, however, break rules and show aggression repeatedly and persistently. Punishment at home or at school doesn't seem to stop them.

Conduct disorder *is* similar to ADHD in that it tends to run in families. It is not caused by poor parenting, even though the parents may also be in trouble with the police and the courts themselves. Twin studies have confirmed that inheritance is a major factor.

Conduct disorder is very difficult to treat. Medications, psychotherapy, and family therapy have all been tried. In one study of children treated at a child-psychiatry clinic in New Zealand, about 90 percent of those with conduct disorder continued to exhibit aggressive, destructive behaviors over the following four years. Conduct disorder doesn't go away over time, and science has not yet found an effective way to lessen its effects.

What is the long-term outlook for children with ADHD?

It used to be thought that children would eventually grow out of ADHD. For many children, the symptoms do lessen during late adolescence and, if they are taking medication, they may be able to manage without it. For other children, however, ADHD lasts into adulthood, and without medication they will continue to struggle with hyperactivity, impulsiveness, and distractibility. At present, no method exists to determine whether any particular child will continue to exhibit the symptoms or will have them as an adult.

Adults with ADHD include successful business people, professionals, academics, artists, sports figures, and criminals. The same could be said of the non-ADHD population. The difference between those who make constructive use of their excess energy and those who get into trouble may well be their experiences as children and adolescents. If they get the help they need to settle down in school, focus on their work, and complete their studies, they have a better chance of making the most of their talents and creativity in productive ways. Those whose problems are neglected, ignored, or inappropriately treated will have a harder time of it.

Most adults with ADHD experience the symptoms in a mild form. They will still tend to be restless, disorganized, distractible, and impulsive. They may procrastinate, or try to do too many things at once and end up finishing none of them. A few have more severe symptoms, such as mood swings, anxiety, frequent bursts of anger, poor self-esteem, and a tendency to take unnecessary risks. They will probably need medication to keep these symptoms under control. Fortunately, there are increasing numbers of physicians, psychologists, and psychiatrists who are knowledgeable about adult ADHD and who can help.

It may be that, as you read this book, you will start to recognize facets of your own behavior. ADHD always begins in childhood, and if the symptoms I've described are those you remember from your own childhood, you may want to talk to a doctor about them. After all, ADHD runs in families and, if you are the parent of a child with ADHD, the likelihood that you have ADHD is greater than that in families without ADHD.

The good news is that every year we learn a little more about ADHD and, as we do, the stigma of this particular disorder seems to lessen a little. If you or your child has ADHD, you will find you are not alone. There are many support groups and places to turn for help. Don't be afraid to reach out.

5

Other Problems That May Affect Learning

"She can read quite well and she doesn't have ADHD, but she's still having trouble keeping up at school, even though she's bright. What's wrong?"

Parents sometimes come to me with this question. They've ruled out a specific learning disorder, and the symptoms of ADHD are not present, yet they know their child is not achieving her potential at school. In this chapter I would like to review various problems that may make it difficult for children to keep up at school.

Teachers, too, may be baffled by a child who seems intelligent and yet can't seem to keep up in class. The problems described in this chapter may provide some clues. If you suspect that a student may have a medical or other problem that interferes with learning, you should ask the parents about it. And, of course, if you are the parent of a child with a known medical problem, you should discuss it with the child's teacher.

"She never speaks up in class."

There are two reasons why a child might be unwilling to talk. It might simply be shyness or the child might be autistic. Although autism is usually diagnosed before a child enters school, some extremely shy children are so tongue-tied at school that teachers suspect autism. Telling the difference is usually a simple matter of asking the right questions in a parent–teacher interview.

Shyness

Children who refuse to speak in strange situations, such as a new school or with a teacher they do not know well, may not have a specific learning disorder, but may be so shy that they appear to be learning-disabled. Extreme shyness is known as "elective mutism."

Sometimes children with this problem are referred to pediatricians to find out if they are autistic. However, it may not be necessary to carry out specialized tests. Simply observe the child carefully. If she speaks normally at home and with close friends, and refuses to speak only in an unfamiliar setting, the problem is most likely shyness.

Most children grow out of this problem eventually. There is little point in trying to coax or bribe or force the child to talk in situations where he is very uncomfortable, and it may make matters worse. Tell him not to worry, explain the problem to each new teacher, and let him develop at his own pace. He will gradually get used to a new teacher and a new class and be able to speak up. You will probably have to repeat this process at the beginning of each new school year.

Teachers may find it difficult to assess the progress of a child who is very shy. Although the child's written work is likely to be unaffected, she doesn't participate in class discussions and may be unable to make presentations. However, at home, she may happily chat to her parents about what she is doing at school. Together, the teacher and the parents may have to come up with an individual way to evaluate what the child has learned.

Autism

Shyness and autism are sometimes confused, because most autistic children are also unable to speak up in class. However, whereas shyness affects a child only with strangers or in an unfamiliar situation, autism affects a child's behavior every-where—at home, at school, on the playground.

Autism is a developmental disorder that affects the way children process information from their senses. Autistic children have difficulty making sense of the world. According to people with the disorder, information seems to come at them "all at once," and they find it hard to sort out all the sensations of color, light, movement, sound, smell, and feeling into a coherent whole. Autistic children may overreact to their environment in tantrums, or underreact and withdraw completely. These differences may lead to unusual behavior and speech patterns.

Autistic children have difficulty connecting to other people, not just their teachers and classmates, but also their parents, siblings, and relatives. They may not make eye contact or they may move in an unusual way, for example, by flapping their hands for no obvious reason. Some autistic children have problems with any kind of change; they cannot bear it if furniture at home is rearranged or if there is a disruption in routine.

The disorder is usually apparent by the time a child is three years old and it is more common in boys than in girls. It appears to be genetic and is *not* a result of poor parenting, although this explanation used to be common and the myth persists. Researchers have found distinct differences between the brains of children with autism and those without the disorder. Children with autism have a larger number of nerve endings in certain areas of the brain, which may account for their sometimes exaggerated reactions to noise, light, or other stimuli, and for their dislike of change. Since they have difficulty making sense of their environment, change in the environment requires them to go through the whole process of sorting out sensory information all over again.

Autism is sometimes known as "pervasive development disorder" (PDD) because it affects many different facets of development—not just speech, but also behavior, movement, relationships, and learning. The condition is fairly rare and affects about 10 people in 10,000.

Some autistic children may fall behind their classmates in some subjects and yet show brilliance in others, such as mathematics. Some develop a fascination for things that other people find uninteresting. One autistic boy could watch the real-estate channel on television for hours on end, but he wasn't particularly interested in anything else on television. Autistic children may also notice things that others don't. Some become fascinated with specific parts of objects, such as doorknobs, hinges, or handles. One boy could identify the type of car someone drove by the car keys, even if they did not display the car manufacturer's logo. Some autistic children, however, suffer from mental retardation and have a very low IQ level.

If you think your child or a student of yours is autistic, then the child should be seen by a neuro-developmental specialist. In some communities, this will be a child psychiatrist; in others, it will be a specially trained pediatrician. Although most autistic children continue to have problems communicating with other people and handling social situations, there are ways to cope with the disorder, using behavior management, family counseling, special community and school programs, and, occasionally, medication. A review of the long-term outlook for autistic children found that a small proportion of children with autism do grow up to lead relatively normal lives, but at present, there is no "cure" for this disorder.

"He's very talkative, but he can't seem to make friends because he doesn't talk about things other children are interested in."

Children who talk fluently and yet seem to be unable to carry on social conversations with other children may have Asperger's syndrome. This is a mild form of autism. These children develop language skills at the same time as most children, but they lack social skills. They don't know how to say the right thing at the right time. Like autistic children, they have a tendency to become preoccupied with interests that may not appeal to others and they don't like changes in their surroundings or routines. Their unusual behavior makes it hard for them to form friendships with other children and to fit in at school. Rejection by other children may in itself cause further problems.

Although the syndrome was first described in 1944 by a Viennese physician, Hans Asperger, it was included in the *Diagnostic and Statistical Manual for Mental Disorders* only in the latest, 1994, edition. This diagnostic manual lists two main types of behavior that characterize the disorder: "impairment in social interaction," and "restricted repetitive and stereotyped patterns of behavior, interests, and activities," including an "inflexible adherence to specific, nonfunctional routines or rituals."

Like autistic children, children with Asperger's syndrome may be gifted in a particular area. Although they may not be good at social conversations and building relationships, they can be talkative and have a rich vocabulary. Many are extremely bright. It is possible that some of the eccentric and brilliant people who have made important contributions to science and learning suffered from this disorder before science came up with a name for it.

A specialist can help identify the syndrome and suggest ways to help these children. Many children with Asperger's syndrome have been helped with social-skills training, behavior management, and, if they also suffer from intense anxiety, medication. Although some continue to stand apart from their peer group, others do learn to get on with others and form friendships.

"My child can't seem to control his body movements and he sometimes shouts incoherently."

Children with Tourette's disorder make movements and sounds they cannot control. Their arms or legs may jerk, or they may make barking noises or say things that make no sense. These symptoms are known as "motor and verbal tics."

Tourette's disorder is a rare condition that occurs more often in boys than in girls. If affects 3 or 4 children in 10,000. Children with the disorder often have attentional problems, which interfere with their progress at school. In addition, because of their odd behavior, they may be shunned by other children, which affects their self-esteem.

Motor and verbal tics can be controlled with medication, and the attention problems can be treated with stimulant medication such as Ritalin. For a long time it was thought that Ritalin and other stimulants made the condition worse, but recent studies have found that this is not the case and that some children with Tourette's disorder can benefit greatly from the medication.

"My daughter suffers from anxiety that is affecting her schoolwork."

All children get anxious at times. Most children are anxious just before tests or exams, or when they have to make a presentation or participate in a school performance. Children who are having difficulty keeping up with a certain subject may feel anxious about that subject. Children may also feel anxious about going to a new school. Even peer pressure can create anxieties: many children desperately want to fit in and be seen as socially acceptable by other children.

Most of these forms of anxiety are a normal part of growing up. They do not last and require only the understanding and support of parents and teachers. However, a few children do suffer from more intense, longer-lasting forms of anxiety that can interfere with their ability to learn and succeed in school. There are five types of anxiety that call for a more formal approach to helping the child cope.

Separation anxiety

This is the anxiety children feel at having to leave their home and family to spend the day among strangers at school. The problem can usually be managed with behavior-modification techniques. The child must attend school, but will be rewarded for doing so and for showing less anxiety. Anything that might reinforce the anxiety is avoided. Eventually, the child will become more comfortable and familiar with the school environment, and the symptoms should lessen. If the child continues to feel anxious, it may be that the child has a school phobia or a more generalized type of anxiety.

Phobias

Phobias are specific fears such as fear of heights, crowds, confined spaces, or certain animals. Some children suffer from school phobia: school itself frightens them. School phobia, like separation anxiety, can often be dealt with through behavior modification and some individual counseling. Extreme phobias may call for the help of a child psychiatrist.

Social anxiety

This is more a more serious form of anxiety than simple shyness. Whereas shy children do eventually form friendships with people they get to know well, children who suffer from social anxiety are afraid of people, not only at school but on the street, in a shop, or at the park. These children will usually need professional psychiatric help to learn to cope.

Generalized anxiety

This is a condition that starts early in life. The child feels fearful about many things, including school. The anxiety is pervasive and interferes with the child's ability to work, play, and form friendships. Children with generalized anxiety need psychiatric help to overcome this problem.

Severe psychiatric illness

Diseases such as schizophrenia may involve symptoms such as anxiety. Many of these illnesses can be treated with appropriate medication and professional counseling.

"He seems depressed and can't seem to focus."

Depression is not just a problem of adolescents and adults. Children can suffer from depression too.

Mood swings

These are the normal emotional ups and downs of childhood that last a few hours or, at most, one or two days. When children enter adolescence, hormones may make the mood swings more exaggerated, but they are still a normal part of growing up. These bouts of gloominess don't require treatment, just patience and understanding. Remember the frustrations and setbacks in your own childhood and be prepared to be sympathetic when your children or students are down in the dumps.

Depression following a loss or failure

Bereavement, moving to a different city or town, failing an important exam or losing a sports event, or performing badly in a public event such as a speech or concert may make a child sad for several weeks at a time. For most children, the depression does not affect their performance at school, but some find it hard to concentrate and their schoolwork suffers. If the child does not get over the loss or failure within a few weeks, and the depression is seriously affecting academic performance, it may be necessary to consult a specialist.

Chronic depression

Depression that lasts more than a few weeks and has no obvious cause, such as a loss or failure, usually will affect the child's schoolwork and requires consultation with a child psychiatrist or psychologist.

Suicidal thoughts

Many children have these kinds of thought occasionally without showing any other signs of serious depression. The thoughts do not affect their relationships, energy level, or schoolwork. The child may not mention these thoughts to a teacher or parent, but, if he does, the parent or teacher should pay attention and let the child talk about them. Listen for the answers to the following questions:

- What event might have triggered the thoughts?
- Has the child simply thought about the possibility of suicide or has he actually formed specific plans?
- Was the child influenced by another child who also has suicidal thoughts, or even strong suicidal tendencies?

When you know a little more about the situation, offer help:

- Is there something that the parent or teacher can do to help him feel better about himself?
- Would he like to talk to a doctor or counselor about the problem?

In most cases, you can tell the child that many other children have the same problem and that there is nothing to worry about. If you are concerned that the problem is serious, however, you may want to arrange for the child to see a child psychiatrist or psychologist.

Constant suicidal ideas or suicidal gestures

Any child who thinks constantly about suicide, makes actual plans for suicide (alone or with another child), or carries out a suicide attempt should be referred to a child psychiatrist immediately.

"She had a lot of ear infections as a child. Could that cause learning problems?"

Back in the 1960s, a few studies proposed a connection between repeated ear infections when children were preschoolers and language problems that led to later learning difficulties. Some of these studies also suggested that preschoolers who attended daycare had more ear infections than those who were cared for at home.

Reviews of the research in the 1980s found no convincing evidence of a connection between ear infections and learning difficulties. They did, however, notice that learning difficulties were related to the level of education of the parents. The children of well-educated parents tend to do better than the children of parents with lower levels of education, even if the children spend more time in daycare and have more ear infections.

"Could his allergies be affecting his performance at school?"

Allergies in themselves do not affect a child's ability to learn, but some antihistamines prescribed for allergies can make children sleepy, which can make it hard for a child to concentrate in school. If your child has allergies, make sure that your doctor prescribes a non-sedating form of antihistamine.

"My child has asthma. Will it affect her ability to keep up in class?"

Asthma itself has no connection to learning difficulties, but, like any chronic medical problem, it can interfere with a child's schooling. Children with asthma that is not treated adequately may miss a lot of school. The more they are absent, the harder they find it to keep up.

An asthma medication called Theophylline was also thought to make it hard for children to concentrate, creating problems similar to ADHD. However, randomized controlled trials by researchers in Ottawa showed that there were no differences between children's attentiveness when they received Theophylline or when they were given a placebo. In any case, there are many alternatives to Theophylline for a child with asthma, so medication should not interfere with the child's learning.

"My son was born prematurely. Will he have trouble at school as a result?"

Premature or preterm birth is a birth that takes place before the end of thirty-seven weeks of pregnancy. It occurs in about 10 percent of pregnancies. Children who are born prematurely may have health problems. They may also have more learning problems than those who were full-term at birth. These problems may be the result of the premature birth itself, or they may be caused by events in the first few weeks of life. Because premature newborns are so tiny and fragile, they are at risk of respiratory problems, which can deprive the brain of oxygen, leading to long-term problems with learning.

Studies such as the Infant Health and Development Program in the United States have focused on environmental factors in premature and low-birthweight babies. Many low-birthweight babies are born to women who are poor, single, teenaged, and with low levels of education. They may not be able to feed or care for their babies properly, which means that the child is doubly disadvantaged. Some may have ADHD themselves, which increases the likelihood that the child will also have ADHD. In particular, children who are neglected—

that is, their parents don't play games with them or encourage them to talk or offer them a range of activities to try—may also fall behind in school. Early stimulation of the mind plays a role in later academic performance.

On the other hand, many low-birthweight children who receive good medical care after birth and are properly fed, nurtured, and stimulated by their parents go on to do well. Prematurity or a low birthweight does not automatically mean that a child will have learning problems.

"I've heard that kids with ADHD may actually have hyperthyroidism."

Hyperthyroidism is quite rare. It is caused by an overactive thyroid gland, which produces too much thyroxine. The condition makes children fidgety, anxious, and nervous, like ADHD, but it has many additional symptoms that are not typical of ADHD. Because all the body processes are speeded up, it can cause a rapid heartbeat. Children feel warm all the time, even on a cool day. They may lose weight and be unable to sleep. Sometimes they have protruding eyes.

A study currently under way at the Hospital for Sick Children in Toronto, led by Dr. Joanne Rovet, is investigating the connection between thyroid function and learning disabilities. The study is also looking at hypothyroidism, which is the opposite of hyperthyroidism and caused by a shortage of thyroxine, makes children slow and lethargic. Children with this condition feel the cold acutely, gain weight, and sometimes have puffy faces. Because of their condition, they may do poorly in school. Like hyperthyroidism, hypothyroidism is rare.

It is very unlikely that children with learning disorders have either of these conditions, but if you see the symptoms of hyper- or hypothyroidism, it is a simple matter to test thyroid function.

"My child has chronic health problems. How will this affect her schoolwork in the long term?"

Any health problem that keeps a child out of school for long periods will affect the child's ability to keep up. Chronically ill children usually need special tutoring or some other form of extra help with schoolwork. However, teachers and parents also need to know about learning problems caused either by the health problems themselves or by the treatments used to combat them.

If you are the parent of a chronically ill child, discuss the problems with your child's teacher so that together you can develop appropriate educational strategies. If you are the teacher of a child who appears to have serious health problems, ask the parents about the nature of the problems so that you can respond appropriately to the child's needs.

Cancer

Certain cancer therapies, such as brain irradiation, or chemotherapy, in which very strong chemicals are injected into the spinal canal, may cause learning problems. Irradiation of parts of the body other than the brain, or chemotherapy that involves intravenous injections, do not affect learning. If your child is diagnosed with cancer, ask about the form of treatment that is proposed and about its long-term effects on the child's learning abilities.

Diabetes

Diabetes that is properly controlled with insulin and diet therapy should not cause learning problems. However, if the diabetes is not under control, and the child has blood sugar levels that are too high or too low, he or she may do poorly in school. If your child has diabetes, make sure that he or she is receiving proper treatment and following any prescribed diet very carefully.

Heart disease

Children with cyanotic congenital heart disease ("blue babies") may have learning problems, but research suggests that these problems will clear up after appropriate surgery.

Epilepsy

Children with the form of epilepsy known as "petit mal" may sometimes be mistaken for children with ADHD. Their seizures do not take the form of obvious convulsions. They do not fall down or shake. Instead, the child suddenly appears to be daydreaming. Her face goes blank and her eyelids may flicker. The episode last only about half a minute, and then she is back to normal. She will be unaware that anything has happened. If a child has these "absence seizures" many times during the day, the teacher is like to wonder if the child has an attentional problem.

"Petit mal" epilepsy is much less common than ADHD. The periods of inattention are brief, not constant, and they are not accompanied by hyperactive or impulsive behavior. Because the symptoms are quite subtle, in some cases "petit mal" epilepsy has gone undiagnosed for some years. The child may complain of tiredness, but seems otherwise fairly healthy.

Epilepsy can be diagnosed by a physician, who will probably order an electroencephalogram (EEG) test and may prescribe anti-seizure drugs. The problem rarely lasts past late adolescence, so the child will not have to take drugs all her life.

Some of the drugs used to prevent serious convulsions and

seizures in children with "grand mal" epilepsy, have been known to affect children's concentration. If your child has epilepsy, discuss any problems your child is having in school with the physician, so that the anticonvulsants with the fewest side effects can be used.

Brain damage or brain injury

A motor-vehicle accident or an infection such as meningitis may cause permanent changes in a child's brain function. In serious cases, the injuries will affect all areas of development; in milder cases, they may leave the child with learning or attentional difficulties. The parents will need to consult with a specialist about appropriate types of treatment.

Cleft lip or cleft palate

Children born with a cleft lip or cleft palate may have difficulty making themselves understood. Surgical repair of the lip and palate not only improves their speech, but also makes the children feel more attractive, which is good for their self-esteem. Unless the problem is associated with additional birth defects that affect the brain, these children do as well as any other children in terms of their ability to learn and to concentrate.

"He always seems so clumsy. Could he have dyspraxia?"

I seem to be hearing this question more often lately. "Dyspraxia" is used to label children who are uncoordinated, or who have difficulty with sorting out right and left, or who find it hard to copy down information from the blackboard. In fact, children with almost any problem relating to movement—from difficulty learning to ride a bicycle to messy eating habits to an inability to hit a baseball—tends to get called dyspraxic these days. I call it the "diagnosis du jour."

I don't use the word "dyspraxia," because it doesn't have any agreed-upon meaning and because I don't think any useful purpose is served by putting a fancy Greek label on children who may have quite minor problems. Yes, indeed, some children are quite clumsy. Some children are bad at sports. Motor control comes more quickly to some children than to others. The amount of time it takes for "normal" children to develop certain skills can vary quite widely. But there is no evidence that clumsy children have a clinical disorder that requires some type of formal intervention. Some clumsy children do extremely well in school, whereas some gifted athletes or talented artists with excellent coordination have learning problems.

Let's not be in a rush to label children as disordered who are simply a little different. Instead of coming up with new names for every conceivable variation in behavior, it might be better to expand our definition of normal behavior. Sometimes specialists, who spend their lives studying and talking to children with learning problems, lose sight of the fact that the large majority of children do not suffer from any learning problems at all. It's easy to start seeing problems where none exists. As a consultant, I have many children referred to me because of clumsiness or other minor variations from the norm. I find it extremely gratifying to be able to "cure" these children by pointing out the broad range of normality, that these children are clearly within this normal range, and that they have many strengths and talents about which they and their parents should be proud. The world has enough real problems, we don't need to invent new ones.

6

You Are Not Alone

Today, the future for children with learning disabilities is brighter than it has ever been. Although science has still a long way to go in understanding the intricacies of brain function and the causes of learning disabilities, we do know how to treat most children with learning or attentional disorder effectively.

None of the treatments is a "cure." There is no magic pill that will make learning disabilities go away. The treatments require the time and patience of parents and teachers, consultations with doctors and special-education specialists, and perhaps the help of a child psychologist. They also take time and persistence to show results. Helping a child with a learning disability cope and succeed at school is a team effort: it takes many people and it is, without question, an effort.

As the parent of a child with a learning disability, you should be prepared to work with others in creating a learning plan for the child and carrying it out. You should never feel that you have to do everything yourself. However, you will have to ask for help. You will need to be an advocate for your child, to make sure he or she gets the best help available at school and from the medical establishment. In some cases, the child's physician may help act as an additional advocate for the child. It is a role I have played many times myself.

Parents also need to learn as much as possible about the child's disorder. Reading this book is a start, and there are suggestions for finding more information in the next chapter. You must know what to ask doctors and teachers, and you must be able to help your child understand why he or she is having problems.

Teachers, too, need to understand many different types of learning disorders, since they are likely to encounter most types over the course of their careers. In a recent survey of teachers in Canada and the United States, researchers found that most teachers had little or no formal education in the area of ADHD at teacher's college or university, and minimal training during professional-development days after graduation. Yet almost all teachers said they wanted to know more and to understand the problems better.

The study also found that about 80 percent of the teachers thought that they had taught children who had undiagnosed ADHD. The same proportion said that they had never talked to an outside professional, such as a medical doctor, about a student's difficulties at school. Only a third understood that the condition is inherited, and most, but not all, knew that it was not the result of poor parenting. Unfortunately, most teachers also believed that the condition could be controlled with diet, which is not the case.

Since the role of the teacher in helping a child with a learning disability is so crucial, it is unfortunate that so few teachers have formal education in this area. There should be a required course on learning and attentional disabilities offered by every teacher-training program.

Not only must teachers overcome any gaps in their training, but, today, they must also deal with cutbacks, larger classes, and a shortage of assistants and special-education resources. Because of these problems, the involvement of the school principal is usually required in developing any individualized education plan. The principal usually has to approve such things as sending a child with dyslexia to a resource room for extra tutoring in phonics, or allowing a child who has difficulties writing to take an examination orally.

Both teachers and parents may get additional support from associations for people with learning disorders or ADHD. These associations have information about the key people within the school system who have the skills and willingness to help children with learning disorders, and about professionals who can help. Parents can also get support from the parents of other children with learning problems and can learn about what has or has not worked for other families. The names of key associations are listed in the next chapter.

The key to success in preparing and carrying out an individualized education plan (IEP) is regular, frequent contact between the parents and the teacher. Teachers and parents should share and discuss the results of all tests, medical, psychological, or academic. Both should monitor the student's progress regularly and ensure that the student is getting the program agreed upon in the IEP. Over the course of the year, the demand on the available resources may increase, which may mean that a child is not getting as much individual attention as he or she was at the beginning of the year, so adjustments may be needed. Parents should also let teachers know about medication schedules for children who are taking stimulant medication for ADHD and teachers should provide feedback if the medication starts to wear off during class, causing a rebound effect.

Be patient. Don't panic if progress is sometimes slow. If a child has fallen behind at school, it will take time for him or her to catch up. I've tried to stress in this book that there are no miracle solutions to learning and attentional disorders, although there are many books and articles peddling products that claim to solve learning problems instantly.

Above all, help the child to feel good about his or her progress, and hopeful about the future. Children long to be accepted and praised. Your positive attitude and encouragement are essential ingredients in any treatment.

7

Getting More Information

When you first start to investigate any learning disorder, you will probably be overwhelmed with the amount of information available. There are dozens of books and thousands of Web sites dealing with dyslexia, ADHD, and other learning problems. Some contain personal accounts of people who have overcome learning problems, and you may find them encouraging, even inspiring. Others are written by people with an ax to grind or something to sell. There are also some books written by doctors and researchers that may help you learn more about learning disorders.

Organizations

If you are the parent of a child with a learning disorder, perhaps you should start by contacting one of the national organizations of people with learning disorders. Groups such as the Learning Disabilities Association of Canada or Children and

Adults with ADD (CHADD) can put you in touch with other parents who are going through what you are going through and can provide advice and encouragement. Of course, parents are not doctors. Some may recommend approaches that I have criticized in this book, but most will be as committed as you are to finding effective, proven methods of helping children.

Learning Disabilities Association of Canada
National Office
323 Chapel Street, Suite 200
Ottawa, Ontario
K1N 7Z2
Telephone: (613) 238-5721
Fax: (613) 235-5391
E-mail: ldactaac@fox.nstn.ca
Web site: http://educ.queensu.ca/~lda/indexe.htm

There are branches of the association in every province and territory. Contact the national office to find the nearest office to your home.

Children and Adults with ADD (CHADD)
8181 Professional Place, Suite 201
Landover, Maryland, U.S.A. 20785
(800) 233-4050 or (301) 306-7070
Fax: (301) 306-7090
Web site: http://members.tripod.com/~chaddcanada/index.html

This is an American organization which has had Canadian chapters since 1991. There are currently chapters in Alberta, British Columbia, New Brunswick, Ontario, Quebec, and Saskatchewan. The Vancouver chapter has a very informative Web site (http://www.vcn.bc.ca/chaddvan). The objectives of the organization are

1. to maintain a support group for families of those with ADHD;
2. to provide a forum for the continuing education of families concerning ADHD;
3. to be a community resource for information about ADHD;
4. to provide educational programs to individuals within the fields of medicine and education so that they may more easily recognize children with ADHD and, thus, provide appropriate treatment and develop appropriate educational programs for those children.

The International Dyslexia Association (formerly The Orton Dyslexia Society)
British Columbia Branch
523-409 Granville Street
Vancouver, B.C. V6C 1T2
Telephone: (604) 669-5811
Fax: (604) 669-5343

The IDA is an international, non-profit, scientific and educational organization dedicated to the study and treatment of dyslexia. At present, the only Canadian branch is in British Columbia.

The ADDO Foundation
Box 223, Station R
Toronto, Ontario
M4G 3Z9
Telephone: (416) 813-6858
Fax: (416) 488-3743
E-mail: ADDO@addofoundation.org
The mandate of the ADDO Foundation is

1. to create greater and appropriate awareness of ADHD and the effect upon children and adults;

2. to advocate to the educational system so that ADHD becomes officially recognized throughout the province as having learning components. Teachers would be trained in ADHD management through undergraduate preservice. Inservice program training is established for both the public and private school systems;

3. to advocate for change to health-care professionals for a standard of care regarding diagnosis and treatment, ensuring they become uniform and multidimensional, and to encourage a greater number of professionals to become trained for this process.

Recommended reading

I wrote this book because I was not completely satisfied with existing books on the market. Some are helpful, but out of date, others are more up-to-date, but are not rigorously based on scientific information. Nevertheless, there are several that provide a useful perspective on learning disorders. Here are a few that are considered generally reliable.

Russell A. Barkley, *Taking Charge of ADHD: The Complete, Authoritative Guide for Parents.* New York: Guilford Press, 1995.
    Russell Barkley is a well-known researcher in this field. His book emphasizes behavior modification and coping skills, but includes some information on medication.

Edward M. Hallowell and John J. Ratey, *Driven to Distraction: Recognizing and Coping with Attention Deficit Disorder from Childhood through Adulthood.* New York: Pantheon Books, 1994.
    This book tells the stories of people with ADHD and focuses on the experience of living with the disorder. There is

more information about diagnosis than about treatment, but it provides reassurance to families and a useful list for teachers containing fifty tips on the classroom management of ADHD.

Barbara Ingersoll and Sam Goldstein, *Attention Deficit Disorder and Learning Disabilities: Realities, Myths and Controversial Treatments*. New York: Doubleday, 1993.

Solid information, with a scientific base, and clearly written. The information is now a few years out of date, but it is still a useful book.

Mark Selikowitz, *Dyslexia and Other Learning Disorders: The Facts*. Melbourne: Oxford University Press, 1998.

One of a series of books about learning disorders, first published in 1993. Reliable and readable.

Larry B. Silver, *The Misunderstood Child: Understanding and Coping with Your Child's Learning Disabilities*, third edition. New York: Random House, 1998.

Written by a child and adolescent psychiatrist who had learning problems as a child. I consider some of his ideas on behavior modification unnecessarily severe, and he recommends certain medications for ADHD that have not yet been studied in large randomized controlled trials. However, he does have useful information for parents of adolescents and for adults with learning disorders.

Information on the Internet

Internet addresses tend to go out of date very quickly, so I won't give you a list of Web sites. If you are familiar with the Internet, use it to find the local branch of the associations listed above. If you don't know how to use the Internet, a librarian at a public library can usually help. You can also get information from Health Canada, and the National Institute of Mental Health in the United States.

The key to using any information from the Internet is to take a critical look at the source of any information you find. There is solid information from science journals and promotional hype from hucksters. You probably won't find it hard to know which is which.

You may also want to join a chat group of parents or teachers who are dealing with the same problems you are. If you live in an isolated area, it will help you stay connected.

Journals

If you are a teacher, you may want to see copies of the *Journal of Learning Disabilities*. I have cited a number of articles from the journal in this book. There are actually two journals with the same name, one American and one British. It is the American one that I have used in my work. If you cannot find copies in a local library, you may want to contact the publisher:

Journal of Learning Disabilities
Pro-Ed Publishers
8700 Shoal Creek Boulevard
Austin, Texas, 78757-6897
Telephone: (512) 451-3246
Fax: (512) 451-8542

References

Chapter 2 Dyslexia and Reading Problems

For a good overview of the current state of research on dyslexia, see Sally E. Shaywitz, "Dyslexia," *New England Journal of Medicine* 338/5 (1998): 307–12.

Studies of identical twins: J.M. Finucci, "Genetic Considerations in Dyslexia," in *Progress in Learning Disabilities*, vol. 4, ed. Helmer R. Myklebust. New York: Grune and Stratton, 1978.

Genetic study at the University of Colorado: J.C. DeFries and Sadie N. Decker, "Genetic Aspects of Reading Disability: A Family Study," in *Reading Disorders: Varieties and Treatments*, ed. R.N. Malatesta and P.G. Aaron. New York: Academic Press, 1982.

Studies of the brains of people with dyslexia using MRI: J.M. Rumsey, R. Dorwart, M. Verness, M.B. Denckla, M.J.P. Kruesi, and J.L. Rapoport, "Magnetic Resonance Imaging of Brain Anatomy in Severe Developmental Dyslexia," *Archives of Neurology* 43 (1986): 1045–46; C. Njiokiktjiei, L. de Sonneville, and J. Vall, "Callosal Size in Children with Learning Disabilities," *Behavioral Brain Research* 64 (1994): 213–18.

Debate about whole language approach versus phonics approach to teaching reading: see, for example, Nicholas Lemann, "The Reading Wars," *Atlantic Monthly*, November 1997, 128–34; or Steve Truch, *The Missing Parts of Whole Language*. Calgary: Foothills Educational Materials, 1991.

Study by Helene Palatajko at the University of Western Ontario: Helene Palatajko, "A Critical Look at Vestibular Dysfunction in Learning-Disabled Children," *Developmental Medicine and Child Neurology* 27 (1985): 283–92.

Studies on light in classrooms: John Ott, "Influence of Fluorescent Lights on Hyperactivity and Learning Disabilities," *Journal of Learning Disabilities* 9 (1976): 417–22; K. Daniel O'Leary, Alan Rosenbaum, and Philip Hughes, "Fluorescent Lighting: A Purported Source of Hyperactive Behavior," *Journal of Abnormal Child Psychology* 6 (1978): 285–89.

Study using an ion generator in the classroom: L.L. Morton and John R. Kershner, "Negative Air Ionization Improves Memory and Attention in Learning-Disabled and Mentally Retarded Children," *Journal of Abnormal Child Psychology* 12 (1984): 353–66.

For more information about the history and misuse of IQ tests, see: Stephen Jay Gould, *The Mismeasure of Man*, rev. ed. New York, Norton, 1996; and Charles Locurto, *Sense and Nonsense about IQ: The Case for Uniqueness*. New York: Praeger, 1991.

Study by Linda Siegel at the Ontario Institute for Studies in Education: Linda Siegel, "Evidence that IQ Scores Are Irrelevant to the Definition and Analysis of Reading Disability," *Canadian Journal of Psychology* 42 (1988): 201–15.

Study by Rachel Gittelman and Ingrid Feingold at Columbia University: Rachel Gittelman and Ingrid Feingold, "Children with Reading Disorders—I. Efficacy of Reading Remediation," *Journal of Child Psychology and Psychiatry* 24/2 (1983): 167–91.

Study of computer-assisted learning at Florida State University: Kathryn Jones, Joseph Torgesen, and Molly Sexton, "Using Computer Guided Practice to Increasing Decoding Fluency in Learning Disabled Children: A Study Using the Hint and Hunt I Program," *Journal of Learning Disabilities* 20 (1987): 122–28.

Study of computer-assisted learning at the University of Colorado: Barbara Wise and Richard K. Olson, "Computer Speech and the Remediation of Reading and Spelling Problems," *Journal of Special Education Technology* 12/3 (1994): 207–20.

Texas study of biofeedback: John Carter and Harold Russell, "Use of EMG Biofeedback Procedures with Learning Disabled Children in a Clinical and Educational Setting," *Journal of Learning Disabilities* 18 (1985): 213–16.

Calgary study of relaxation techniques: T.H. Zieffle and D.M. Romney, "Comparison of Self-Instruction and Relaxation Training in Reducing Impulsive and Inattentive Behavior of Learning Disabled Children on Cognitive Tasks," *Psychological Reports* 57 (1985): 271–74.

Statement by the American Academy of Pediatrics, the American Association of Pediatric Ophthalmology and Strabismus, and the American Academy of Ophthalmology about Irlen lenses and eye exercises: the statement has been posted on the World Wide Web at http://www.aap.org/policy/re9825.html. It cites many of the research papers that demonstrate the ineffectiveness of these alternative therapies.

Test of sensory integration therapies: E. Carte, D. Morrison, J. Sublett, A. Uemura, and W. Setrakian, "Sensory Integration Therapy: A Trial of a Specific Neurodevelopmental Therapy for the Remediation of Learning Disabilities," *Journal of Developmental Behaviour Pediatrics* 5 (1984): 189–194.

Statement by the American Association of Pediatrics about patterning/the Doman-Delacato method: American Association of Pediatrics, "The Doman-Delacato Treatment of Neurologically Handicapped Children," *Pediatrics* 70 (1982): 810–12.

Follow-up studies: The studies mentioned are cited and described in Barbara Maughan, "Annotation: Long-Term Outcomes of Developmental Reading Problems," *Journal of Child Psychology and Psychiatry* 36/3 (1995): 357–71.

Chapter 3   Writing, Spelling, and Math Problems

Study on poor spellers by researchers in Maryland and Montana: Karen R. Harris, Steve Graham, and Sally Freeman, "Effects of Strategy Training on Metamemory among Learning Disabled Students," *Exceptional Children* 54 (1988): 332–38.

Study on number of children suffering from a math disability: Varda Gross-Tsur, Orly Manor, and Ruth S. Shalev, "Developmental Dyscalculia: Prevalence and Demographic Features," *Developmental Medicine and Child Neurology* 38 (1996): 25–33.

Study on children who had average reading ability and math disability: Linda Siegel and William Feldman, "Nondyslexic Children with Combined Writing and Arithmetic Learning Disabilities," *Clinical Pediatrics* 22/4 (1983): 241–44.

Study on children with math disability that cannot be traced to reading or attentional problems: Clive Lewis, Graham J. Hitch, and Peter Walker, "The Prevalence of Specific Arithmetic Difficulties and Specific Reading Difficulties in 9- to 10-year-old Boys and Girls," *Journal of Child Psychology and Psychiatry* 35/2 (1994): 283–92.

Chapter 4 Attention Deficit Hyperactivity Disorder

Surveys of teachers on numbers of children who have ADHD: Ronald L. Trites, "Prevalence of Hyperactivity in Ottawa, Canada," in *Hyperactivity in Children: Etiology, Measurement and Treatment Implications*, ed. Ronald L. Trites. Baltimore: University Park Press, 1979.

Children with ADHD who also have a specific learning disorder: P.L. Holborrow and P.S. Berry, "Hyperactivity and Learning Difficulties," *Journal of Learning Disabilities* 19 (1986): 426–31.

Twin studies and studies of adopted children: Reviewed in Lily Hechtman, "Genetic and Neurobiological Aspects of Attention Deficit Hyperactivity Disorder: A Review," *Journal of Psychiatry and Neuroscience* 19/3 (1994): 193–201.

Studies on children who benefit from stimulant medication, provided that doses are adjusted: Reviewed in Josephine Elia, Paul J. Ambrosini, and Judith L. Rapoport, "Treatment of Attention Deficit Hyperactivity Disorder," *New England Journal of Medicine* 340/10 (1999): 780–88.

Studies on stimulant use and school performance: Josephine Elia, Patricia A. Welsh, Charles S. Gullota, and Judith L. Rapoport, "Classroom Academic Performance: Improvement with Both Methylphenidate and Dextroamphetamine in ADHD Boys," *Journal of Child Psychology and Psychiatry* 34/5 (1993): 785–804; see also review of several studies in Josephine Elia, Paul J. Ambrosini, and Judith L. Rapoport, "Treatment of Attention Deficit Hyperactivity Disorder," *New England Journal of Medicine* 340/10 (1999): 780–88.

Long-term study in Sweden: Christopher Gillberg, Hans Melander, Anne-Liis von Knorring, Lars-Olof Janols, Gunilla Thernlund, Bruno Hägglöf, Lena Eidevall-Wallin, Peik Gustafson, and Svenny Kopp, "Long-Term Stimulant Treatment of Children with Attention Deficit Hyperactivity Disorder Symptoms," *Archives of General Psychiatry* 54 (1997): 857–64.

Study on stimulant use and self-esteem: Patrick Kelly, Melvin Cohen, William Walker, Owen Caskey, and A.W. Atkinson, "Self-Esteem in Children Medically Managed for Attention Deficit Disorder," *Pediatrics* 83 (1989): 211–17.

Study on stimulant use and relationships with other children: Charles Cunningham, Linda Siegel, and David Offord, "A Developmental Dose-Response Analysis of the Effects of Methylphenidate on the Peer Interactions of Attention Deficit Disordered Boys," *Journal of Child Psychology and Psychiatry* 26 (1985): 955–71.

Study on stimulant use and relationships with teachers: Carol Whalen, Barbara Henker, and Sharon Dotemoto, "Teacher Response to the Methylphenidate (Ritalin) versus Placebo Status of Hyperactive Boys in the Classroom," *Child Development* 52 (1981): 1005–14.

Study on stimulant use and family relationships: Russell Barkley and Charles Cunningham, "The Effects of Methylphenidate on the Mother–Child Interactions of Hyperactive Children," *Archives of General Psychiatry* 36 (1979): 201–8.

Long-term studies on stimulant use and growth: Mortimer Gross, "Growth of Hyperkinetic Children taking Methylphenidate, Dextroamphetamine, or Imipramine/Desipramine," *Pediatrics* 58 (1976): 423–31.

Studies in Baltimore County: Daniel Safer and John Krager, "Trends in Medication Treatment of Hyperactive Schoolchildren," *Clinical Pediatrics* 22 (1983): 500–4; Daniel Safer and John Krager, "The Increased Use of Stimulant Treatment for Hyperactive/Inattentive Students in Secondary Schools," *Pediatrics* 94 (1994): 462–64.

Long-term studies on stimulant use and drug abuse in later life: Lily Hechtman, "Adolescent Outcome of Hyperactive Children Treated with Stimulants in Childhood: A Review," *Psychopharmacology Bulletin* 21 (1995): 178–91; Timothy E. Wilens, Joseph Biederman, Thomas J. Spencer, and Richard J. Frances, "Comorbidity of Attention Deficit Hyperactivity and Psychoactive Substance Abuse Disorders," *Hospital and Community Psychiatry* 45 (1994): 421–25.

Report by the American Medical Association in response to the perceived overprescribing of stimulant drugs for ADHD: Larry Goldman, Myron Genel, Rebecca Bezman, and Priscilla Slanetz, "Diagnosis and Treatment of Attention-Deficit/Hyperactivity Disorder in Children and Adolescents," *Journal of the American Medical Association* 279/14 (1998): 1100–7.

Study on behavior-management approach: Howard Abikoff and Rachel Gittelman, "Does Behavior Therapy Normalize the Classroom Behavior of Hyperactive Children?" *Archives of General Psychiatry* 41 (1984): 449–54.

Studies comparing stimulant treatment to behavior modification: Philip Firestone, M.J. Kelly, T. Goodman, and J. Davey, "Differential Effects of Parent Training and Stimulant Medication with Hyperactives," *Journal of the American Academy of Child and Adolescent Psychiatry* 20 (1981): 135–47; Rachel Gittelman Klein and Howard Abikoff, "The Role of Psychostimulants and Psychosocial Treatments in Hyperkinesis," in *Attention Deficit Disorder: Clinical and Basic Research*, ed. Terje Sagvolden and Trevor Archer. Hillsdale: L. Erlbaum Associates, 1989.

Studies on lack of social skills: Stephanie H. McConaughty and David R. Ritter, "Social Competence and Behavioral Problems of Learning Disabled Boys," *Journal of Learning Disabilities* 19 (1986): 39–45; Charles Cunningham, Linda Siegel, and David Offord, "A Developmental Dose-Response Analysis of the Effects of Methylphenidate on the Peer Interactions of Attention Deficit Disordered Boys," *Journal of Child Psychology and Psychiatry* 26 (1985): 955–71.

Study comparing the effects of social-skills training and academic training: John Coie and Gina Krehbiel, "Effects of Academic Tutoring on the Social Status of Low-Achieving, Socially Rejected Children," *Child Development* 55 (1984): 1465–78.

Study on sugar and hyperactivity: Richard Milich and William Pelham, "Effects of Sugar Ingestion on the Classroom and Playgroup Behaviour of Attention Deficit Disordered Boys," *Journal of Consulting and Clinical Psychology* 54 (1986): 714–18.

Study on mothers' beliefs that sugar causes hyperactivity: Daniel Hoover and Richard Milich, "Effects of Sugar Ingestion Expectancies on Mother–Child Interactions," *Journal of Abnormal Child Psychology* 22 (1994): 501–15.

"A new form of child abuse": Pasquale Accardo, "The Myth of Homo Gastronomicus: Your Child Is Not What He Eats," *Missouri Medicine* 82 (1985): 72–74.

Review of Feingold diet: Esther Wender, "The Food Additive–Free Diet in the Treatment of Behavioral Disorders: A Review," *Developmental and Behavioral Pediatrics* 7 (1986): 35–42.

Study on megavitamin therapy: Robert Haslam, J. Thomas Dalby, and Alfred W. Rademaker, "Effects of Megavitamin Therapy on Children with Attention Deficit Disorders," *Pediatrics* 74 (1984): 103–11.

Study on essential fatty acids: Michael G. Aman, Edwin A. Mitchell, and Sarah H. Turbott, "The Effects of Essential Fatty Acid Supplementation by Efamol in Hyperactive Children," *Journal of Abnormal Child Psychology* 15/1 (1987): 75–90.

Study on conduct disorder: David M. Fergusson, L. John Horwood, and Michael T. Lynskey, "The Effects of Conduct Disorder and Attention Deficit in Middle Childhood on Offending and Scholastic Ability at age 13," *Journal of Childhood Psychology and Psychiatry* 34/6 (1993): 899–916.

Chapter 5 Other Problems That May Interfere with Learning

Ritalin does not worsen Tourette's syndrome: John T. Walkup, "Stimulant Treatment of Attention Deficit Hyperactivity Disorder in Children and Adolescents with Tourette's Disorder," *Newsletter of the Journal of the American Academy of Child and Adolescent Psychiatry* 25/1 (1994): 248–50.

Studies of Theophylline: Anne Schlieper, Denise Alcock, Pierre Beaudry, William Feldman, and Lewis Leikin, "Effect of Therapeutic Plasma Concentrations of Theophylline on Behavior, Cognitive Processing, and Affect in Children with Asthma," *Journal of Pediatrics* 118 (1991): 449–55.

Problems of premature babies: Ruth T. Gross, Donna Spiker, and Christina W. Haynes, *Helping Low Birth Weight, Premature Babies: The Infant Health and Development Program.* Stanford, CA: Stanford University Press, 1997.

Hyperthyroidism: Giuseppe Mirabella, Nancy Lobaugh, Sandra Newton, Denice Feig, Elizabeth Astzalos, Kusiel Perlman, and Joanne Rovet, "Effects of Intrauterine Thyroid-Hormone Deficiencies on Attention, Learning and Memory in Infancy," paper presented at First Annual Research in Progress Symposium, the Toronto Fetal Centre, Hospital for Sick Children, Toronto, January 29, 1998.

Chapter 6 You Are Not Alone

Surveys of teachers that found that they did not have formal training in ADHD: Laurence Jerome, Michael Gordon, and Paul Hustler, "A Comparison of American and Canadian Teachers' Knowledge and Attitudes towards Attention Deficit Hyperactivity Disorder (ADHD)," *Canadian Journal of Psychiatry* 39 (1994): 563–67.

Index

Abikoff, Howard, 149
absenteeism, 29
abstract symbols, 100
academic ability tests, 55–56
ADDO Foundation, 192–193
ADHD. *See* attention deficit hyper-
    activity disorder
adult literacy materials, 68
air quality, 45–46
allergen-free diets, 158–160
allergies, 113, 179
alternative therapies, 22–24
American Academy of Allergy and
    Immunology, 158, 160
American Academy of
    Ophthalmology, 75
American Academy of Pediatrics, 75
American Association of Pediatric
    Ophthalmology and Strabismus, 75
American Association of Pediatrics, 78
American Psychiatric Association,
    109, 116
amitriptyline. *See* Elavil
antihypertensive medication, 142
anxiety, 175–176
"applied kinesiology," 79
appropriate treatment, 9–10
Asperger, Hans, 173
Asperger's syndrome, 173–174
asthma, 179–180

attention deficit disorder (ADD).
    See attention deficit hyperactivity
    disorder
*Attention Deficit Disorder and
    Learning Disabilities: Realities,
    Myths and Controversial
    Treatments,* 194
attention deficit hyperactivity disorder,
    50, 52, 55, 86, 88, 96
alternatives to stimulants, 140–142
behaviour modification, 142–152
benefits of medication, 126–127
"borderline" children, 122
causes, 110–112
decision on medication, 137–140
defining the problem, 104–109
and depression, 140–141
diagnosis, 115–123, 122
diet, 112–113
differing definitions of the disorder,
    103–104
distractibility, 106
doctor's opinion, 119–120
family environment, 111–112
gender, 109
and genetics, 111
home environment, 113–115
hyperactivity, 108
impulsiveness, 107–108
inattentiveness, 105–107